Leading Unionized Workforces
in the Age of AI

Leading Unionized Workforces in the Age of AI

Managing Skilled and Unskilled Labor in a Changing World

Nick E. Gilewski

BEP

BUSINESS EXPERT PRESS

Leader in applied, concise business books

Leading Unionized Workforces in the Age of AI:
Managing Skilled and Unskilled Labor in a Changing World

First published in 2025 by
Business Expert Press, LLC
222 East 46th Street, New York, NY 10017
www.businessexpertpress.com

ISBN-13: 978-1-63742-868-9 (paperback)
ISBN-13: 978-1-63742-869-6 (e-book)

Human Resource Management and Organizational Behavior Collection

First edition: 2025

10 9 8 7 6 5 4 3 2 1

EU SAFETY REPRESENTATIVE
Mare Nostrum Group B.V.
Mauritskade 21D
1091 GC Amsterdam
The Netherlands
gpsr@mare-nostrum.co.uk

Description

Managing unionized labor is more complex than ever. The rise of AI, automation, and digital transformation is reshaping industries, redefining job roles, and challenging traditional labor–management dynamics. Leaders must now navigate the intersection of technology, workforce evolution, and unionized labor, ensuring fairness, adaptability, and collaboration in an era of unprecedented change.

In *Leading Unionized Workforces in the Age of AI*, Dr. Nick E. Gilewski offers an insightful and practical roadmap for executives, managers, HR professionals, and union representatives who must lead effectively amid these shifts. Drawing on over two decades of experience in managing skilled and unskilled labor across diverse industries, this book provides a comprehensive guide to leadership, workforce relations, and the future of unionized work.

Key highlights include:

- **Historical and Modern Context:** Explore the evolution of labor unions and how AI, automation, and digitalization are shaping the future of work.
- **Leadership Strategies:** Learn actionable frameworks for managing both skilled and unskilled labor in unionized environments, fostering trust, and enhancing productivity.
- **Real-World Case Studies:** Gain insights from industries such as manufacturing, healthcare, utilities, and construction, showcasing best practices and lessons learned.
- **AI and the Future of Work:** Understand the implications of automation, AI-driven performance tracking, job displacement, and reskilling—and how to navigate these changes with proactive leadership.
- **Workplace Safety and Ethical AI Use:** Discover how AI is influencing safety standards, worker rights, surveillance practices, and ethical concerns—and what leaders must do to maintain a balanced, fair workplace.

Whether you are a supervisor stepping into a unionized environment for the first time, a seasoned executive refining your leadership approach, or a union representative seeking deeper insight into AI's impact on labor relations, this book serves as a must-have guide for the modern workforce.

Leading Unionized Workforces in the Age of AI equips you with the knowledge and tools to build stronger, more collaborative labor–management relationships, ensure worker protections, and lead effectively in the evolving world of work.

Contents

List of Figures and Tables

Figures

Tables

Dedication

To the men and women, I have had the honor of managing and working alongside throughout my career:

Your hard work, resilience, and dedication not only shaped the success of our workplace but also inspired my growth as a leader. Each interaction, challenge, and collaboration contributed to the lessons and experiences that made this book possible.

This is for you—thank you for teaching me the value of integrity, teamwork, and the strength of a united workforce.

Acknowledgments

I want to begin by thanking my wife, Bridget, for her unwavering love and support. You have been my rock through every challenge, and your belief in me means more than words can express. To my children, Brenden, Brianna, and Chandler, you are my inspiration. Your encouragement and pride in my work give me purpose and drive.

To my parents, Bruce and Darleen, I owe so much of who I am today to your guidance and unconditional support. You taught me the value of hard work, honesty, and perseverance, and for that, I am forever grateful.

Foreword 1

As someone who began my career as a union member and eventually rose to a leadership position within the union before transitioning into management, I've had the unique opportunity to experience union dynamics from both sides of the table. Over the years, I've seen how the presence of a strong and effective union can serve as a lifeline for workers, advocating for fair wages, safety, and dignity. At the same time, I've witnessed the challenges faced by those tasked with managing unionized workforces, where every decision carries the weight of a complex, often contentious, relationship.

"Dr. Nick E. Gilewski's *Leading Unionized Workforces in the Age of AI: Managing Skilled and Unskilled Labor in a Changing World* is a refreshing and essential guide for anyone navigating this intricate landscape." What sets this book apart is its objectivity and impartiality. Far from taking sides, Dr. Gilewski provides a balanced perspective that acknowledges both the vital role unions play in ensuring worker rights and the difficulties leaders face in achieving operational excellence while maintaining strong union relationships.

This book is not a critique of unions; nor is it a blueprint for undermining their influence. Instead, it is an honest exploration of how unions and management can coexist and thrive. Dr. Gilewski delves into the history and purpose of unions, shedding light on their evolution and their necessity in industries where worker protections are paramount. From my own time in the union, I can attest to the importance of these protections in fostering a workplace culture where workers feel secure and valued.

But what makes this book truly impactful is its focus on leadership. Dr. Gilewski emphasizes that managing unionized employees requires a unique skill set—a blend of empathy, fairness, and procedural discipline. Through his firsthand experiences, he illustrates how leaders can build trust, navigate grievances, and foster collaboration while respecting the boundaries of union agreements. This is not a one-size-fits-all approach but a nuanced methodology that recognizes the distinct needs of different industries, unions, and workers.

For union members, this book is a valuable resource that demystifies the management perspective. It provides insight into the challenges and responsibilities of leadership, fostering an appreciation for the delicate balance managers must strike to ensure both operational efficiency and worker satisfaction. For managers, it offers practical strategies for cultivating mutual respect and achieving organizational goals without compromising on the principles of fairness and transparency.

As someone who has walked the line between union advocacy and managerial responsibility, I know how difficult it can be to find that equilibrium. *Leading Unionized Workforces in the Age of AI: Managing Skilled and Unskilled Labor in a Changing World* is the guide I wish I had when I first stepped into a leadership role. It equips readers with the tools they need to not only manage but also lead in a way that builds stronger, more productive workplaces.

Whether you are a union member, a supervisor, or an executive tasked with managing unionized labor, this book is a must-read. "Dr. Gilewski's insights are timely, thought-provoking, and grounded in real-world experience." I am confident that the lessons contained within these pages will leave you better prepared to navigate the complexities of union–management dynamics and, ultimately, to foster environments where both workers and organizations can thrive.

Sr. Officer John Wall
United States Customs and Border Protection
Former Union Leader and Management Advocate

Foreword 2

As an x-ray technologist working in a hospital, I've come to deeply appreciate the vital role unions play in ensuring fairness, safety, and dignity in the workplace. From negotiating fair wages to advocating for better working conditions, unions serve as the voice of frontline workers—those of us who care for patients, support families, and respond to crises every day. When I became a union steward, it was because I wanted to do more to support my fellow technologists and make a positive difference in our working environment.

When I first picked up *Leading Unionized Workforces in the Age of AI: Managing Skilled and Unskilled Labor in a Changing World*, I wasn't sure what to expect. As someone who has lived and breathed union dynamics, I thought I knew most of what there was to know. But Dr. Nick E. Gilewski's book surprised me. It didn't just provide a deep dive into the history of unions—much of which I hadn't learned before—it also offered practical, actionable advice on how to foster healthy relationships between management and unions.

What struck me most about this book was its objectivity. "Dr. Gilewski writes with a rare impartiality that respects both the necessity of unions and the challenges of managing them." He talked about a collaborative approach, by developing trust and credibility between management and union. It's a balancing act that isn't easy to achieve. Too often, conversations about unions become divisive, but this book bridges that divide by highlighting the mutual benefits that can arise when union representatives and managers work together in good faith.

I especially appreciated the leadership strategies outlined in the book. They don't just serve management; they also empower unions by ensuring a respectful and productive working relationship. Dr. Gilewski emphasizes fairness, open communication, and a shared commitment to problem-solving—values I wholeheartedly agree with. His emphasis on history also resonated with me; understanding where unions come from is essential to appreciating their importance and relevance today.

As the chief union steward, I am inherently biased toward the value of unions, but I can also recognize that successful union–management relationships require effort and understanding from both sides. This book isn't just a tool for managers; it's a guide for union members, too. It equips us with a greater understanding of what effective leadership looks like and how we can work collaboratively to achieve our shared goals.

If you are a manager, this book will help you navigate the intricacies of labor relations with skill and fairness. If you are a union member, it will remind you of the rich history and enduring necessity of the labor movement while offering insights into how we can build bridges with those in management. In my view, *Leading Unionized Workforces in the Age of AI: Managing Skilled and Unskilled Labor in a Changing World* isn't just a book—it's a roadmap to a more collaborative, equitable future.

"Dr. Gilewski has given us a valuable resource that transcends typical labor–management dynamics. It's a book that I would recommend to anyone invested in fostering a workplace where fairness, respect, and collaboration thrive."

Kristen Fleming
Chief Union Steward, CWA1168
Kaleida Health

Author Quotes

"Great leaders aren't born—they're sculpted. Leadership is a journey of growth, vision, and impact; it begins with the courage to invest in yourself and others."—**Nick E. Gilewski PhD, MSIT, MBA, PMP, CMRP, ACC**

Reviewer Quotes

"Dr. Nick E. Gilewski's Leading Unionized Workforces in the Age of AI: Managing Skilled and Unskilled Labor in a Changing World *is a refreshing and essential guide for anyone navigating this intricate landscape. Dr. Gileweski's insights are timely, thought-provoking, and grounded in real-world experience."*—**Sr. Officer John Wall, United States Customs and Border Protection, Former Union Leader and Management Advocate**

"Dr. Gilewski writes with a rate impartiality that respects both the necessity of unions and the challenges of managing them. Dr. Gilewski has given us a valuable resource that transcends typical labor–management dynamics. It's a book that I would recommend to anyone invested in fostering a workplace where fairness, respect, and collaboration thrive."—**Kristen Fleming, Chief Union Steward, CWA1168, Kaleida Health**

Introduction

Welcome to *Leading Unionized Workforces in the Age of AI: Managing Skilled and Unskilled Labor in a Changing World*, a practical guide for navigating the unique challenges of managing unionized labor across various sectors. This book offers actionable insights, firsthand experiences, and proven strategies to foster balanced, collaborative, and productive relationships between management and unionized employees. By embracing a constructive approach, you can enhance organizational success and reinforce your leadership position while navigating the new realities of artificial intelligence (AI), automation, and workforce evolution.

Managing skilled and unskilled labor is both an art and a science. Skilled labor often brings specialized expertise and high value to an organization, while unskilled labor forms the backbone of essential operations. Each group presents unique challenges and requires a nuanced management approach—one that balances operational efficiency with worker protections. With the rise of AI-driven automation, these dynamics are shifting rapidly, creating new opportunities and challenges for leaders, union representatives, and workers alike.

Dr. Nick E. Gilewski brings a depth of expertise to this complex subject. With a doctoral degree from Niagara University and master's degrees in industrial engineering and business administration, he merges academic insight with over 25 years of real-world experience. He currently serves as an Executive Engineering Manager at Samsung Semiconductor Manufacturing in Austin, Texas, and an adjunct professor at Buffalo State University. His career spans high-tech, manufacturing, and industrial sectors, providing a unique perspective on how labor relations, technology, and AI intersect in the modern workplace.

Drawing from his extensive experience working with unions such as IAM, USW, IOUE, BCT, IBEW, and UWUA, Dr. Gilewski offers readers practical insights into managing unionized employees effectively. His professional background—combined with certifications in Six Sigma Green Belt, Project Management Professional (PMP), Certified

Maintenance Reliability Professional (CMRP), and Associate Certified Coach (ACC)—positions him as a reliable guide for leaders navigating labor–management relations in an era of AI and digital transformation.

This book is not merely theoretical; it is a practical resource informed by real-world experiences. For **managers**, **HR professionals**, and **union leaders**, understanding how AI, automation, and evolving labor laws impact unionized workforces is now a necessity, not an option. With AI-driven performance tracking, job displacement concerns, and digital labor negotiations becoming increasingly common, leaders must adapt their strategies to maintain trust, transparency, and fair treatment while ensuring organizational competitiveness.

In today's evolving industrial landscape, managing unionized labor effectively—whether skilled or unskilled—is more critical than ever. The dynamics of labor relations, AI adoption, and global market pressures call for adept leadership to maintain stability and drive success. This book is divided into four parts, beginning with foundational concepts, followed by Dr. Gilewski's personal experiences, strategic management insights, and practical tools and resources for continuous growth. Whether you are a seasoned professional or new to managing unionized labor, the knowledge and skills shared here will equip you for success in this challenging yet rewarding field.

It is important to note that Dr. Gilewski's perspective on unions is neutral. His emphasis is on understanding union history, dynamics, and evolution to foster effective management. Regardless of personal viewpoints, understanding the complexities of unionized labor relations and their historical development is essential for building productive, balanced workplaces in a technology-driven future.

With AI and automation transforming industries, leaders must be prepared to work alongside both labor unions and technological advancements to create fair, efficient, and forward-thinking workplaces. This book will help you navigate these shifts, ensuring that workers and management alike can adapt, grow, and thrive in an era where human expertise and AI integration must go hand in hand.

Purpose and Scope of the Book

Managing unionized labor is not only about supervising tasks or enforcing contracts—it is a delicate balance of leadership, empathy, negotiation, and an in-depth understanding of both historical and modern labor dynamics. In an era defined by rapid technological change, shifting workforce expectations, and evolving economic landscapes, managing unionized workforces presents both significant challenges and unparalleled opportunities.

The rise of artificial intelligence (AI), automation, and digital transformation is redefining the workforce—changing job roles, skill requirements, and collective bargaining dynamics. These changes are reshaping the way unions and employers interact, demanding a new approach to leadership that considers not just traditional labor relations but also the implications of AI-driven automation, remote work, and emerging labor technologies.

The purpose of this book is to serve as a comprehensive guide *for managers, supervisors, HR professionals, labor relations specialists*, and *business leaders* navigating the intricacies of unionized labor. Whether you are new to a supervisory role or an experienced leader seeking to refine your approach, this book will provide both foundational knowledge and forward-looking strategies. By understanding the history and evolution of unions, drawing from Dr. Gilewski's real-world experience managing unionized teams, and applying modern leadership techniques, you will be prepared to lead confidently and successfully.

This book is divided into four key parts:

- **Part 1—Foundations of Unionized Labor**—provides a historical and structural understanding of unionized labor. It explores the emergence of skilled and unskilled labor, the development of unions, and their evolving role in shaping workplace standards, safety, and economic justice. It also examines how technological advances, including AI, are influencing labor classifications and union strategies, offering essential context for effective leadership in today's changing workforce.

- **Part 2—Personal Journey in Managing Unionized Workforces**—offers a candid look into my personal journey managing unionized workforces across multiple industries—from manufacturing to power generation and utilities. Through these experiences, I share lessons learned, challenges faced, and the practical, actionable strategies that helped me grow as a leader. My hope is that these real-world stories will serve as both inspiration and practical guidance for navigating the complexities of union management.

- **Part 3—Industry Insights and Future Trends**—presents practical strategies for leading unionized teams in a changing environment. It explores the influence of AI and automation on labor relations and offers guidance on how leaders can adopt new technologies while preserving job stability, promoting workforce development, and maintaining union collaboration.

- **Part 4—Conclusion and Additional Resources**—emphasizes professional growth and strategic leadership. It reinforces key lessons, encourages ongoing engagement with union partners, and equips readers with tools to strengthen labor relations. Appendixes include a glossary, sample agreements, management resources, and recommended readings for continued learning.

The scope of this book is broad yet targeted. It provides a comprehensive exploration of union history, workforce management, and emerging labor trends while delivering specific, actionable strategies that can be applied immediately. By sharing real-world challenges and tested solutions, this book equips leaders to build stronger relationships with unionized employees, drive collaboration, and create a thriving work environment that supports both business success and workforce well-being.

By the end of this book, readers will have gained the knowledge, insights, and tools to manage unionized workforces skillfully, embrace both tradition and innovation, and prepare for the future of labor relations in an AI-driven world.

This journey is ultimately about leadership. It is about viewing unionized employees not as adversaries but as essential partners in driving long-term success. Let's get started.

Unions that Dr. Gilewski has had the privilege of managing:

Figure 1.1 *Union emblems of which Dr. Gilewski has managed*

PART 1

Foundations of Unionized Labor

CHAPTER 1

Union History and Understanding Its Role in the Modern Workplace

Only a fool would try to deprive working men and working women of their right to join the union of their choice.

—Dwight D. Eisenhower

The Importance of Understanding Union History

This chapter is valuable for **managers, HR professionals, union stewards**, and **business leaders** seeking to understand the fundamentals of managing unionized skilled labor. It provides an overview of key concepts, the significance of labor relations, and the structure of this book, setting the stage for practical strategies in later chapters.

Just as a skilled tradesman needs to understand how a system works before attempting to fix it, it is essential to grasp the history and evolution of unions before effectively managing them. A thorough knowledge of the past provides valuable insights into the present dynamics and challenges within unionized workplaces. By exploring the historical context, we gain a deeper appreciation of unions' evolving role in advocating for workers' rights. Unions have been a cornerstone of labor and employment history, profoundly shaping the relationship between employers and employees.

The Industrial Revolution and the Rise of Unions

The history of unions is deeply intertwined with the broader narrative of industrialization and economic development. As the Industrial

Revolution gained momentum in the late 18th and early 19th centuries, societies witnessed a seismic shift from agrarian economies to industrial powerhouses such as the United States, Britain, Germany, and France. Factories sprouted up across urban landscapes, heralding a new era of mass production and technological innovation (Hobsbawm 1964).

However, this industrial boom came at a significant human cost. Workers were often subjected to deplorable conditions: They worked long hours in unsafe environments, received meager wages that barely sustained their families, and had little to no job security. Child labor was rampant, and the lack of regulatory oversight meant that employers could exploit workers with impunity. For example, during the early years of the Industrial Revolution in Britain, factory workers, including children as young as 5 years of age, often worked 12- to 16-hour days under dangerous conditions. The lack of safety regulations led to frequent accidents, resulting in severe injuries or deaths. In 1833, the British government conducted an inquiry revealing that many factory workers suffered from chronic illnesses and debilitating injuries due to the harsh working environments, which led to early labor movements (Marwick 1973).

Early Labor Movements and Key Milestones

Against this backdrop of exploitation and hardship, the first labor unions began to form. These early unions were often small, informal groups of workers who shared a common trade or craft. They united out of necessity, driven by a shared desire to improve their working conditions and protect their livelihoods. The developing labor movement faced formidable opposition from both employers and governments. Employers viewed unions as a direct threat to their control over the workforce and their profit margins. A notable example of this was the Homestead Strike of 1892 in the United States. The Carnegie Steel Company, under the management of Henry Clay Frick, fiercely opposed the unionization efforts of its workers. When the Amalgamated Association of Iron and Steel Workers went on strike, Frick hired Pinkerton agents to break the strike, leading to a violent confrontation that resulted in deaths on both sides. The government eventually intervened by sending in the state militia to restore order, siding with the industrial interests and suppressing the union activities through force. This event highlighted the lengths to which employers and the government would go to maintain control and protect industrial profits (Krause 1992). Despite these challenges, the resolve of early unionists never wavered. They were fueled by a vision of a fairer, more just society where workers' rights were respected and protected.

The 8-Hour Workday and the Haymarket Incident

The Haymarket Incident of 1886 was a pivotal and tragic event in U.S. labor history, which occurred on May 4, 1886, in Chicago, Illinois. It began as a peaceful rally in support of workers striking for an 8-hour workday, part of a broader labor movement gaining momentum across the country. The demonstration took place in Haymarket Square, where labor activists, socialists, and anarchists gathered to voice their demands (Avrich 1984).

As the rally was winding down, a group of police officers arrived to disperse the crowd. Suddenly, an unknown individual threw a bomb into the police ranks, killing one officer instantly. The police opened fire on the crowd, and in the ensuing chaos, several police officers and protesters were killed or wounded (Green 2006). The total death toll remains unclear, but seven police officers and four civilians died, with many more injured (Smith 2016).

In the aftermath, public opinion turned sharply against the labor movement, particularly its radical elements, such as anarchists. Eight anarchists were arrested and charged with conspiracy and murder, even though there was little evidence linking them directly to the bombing. Four of them were executed, one committed suicide in jail, and the others were later pardoned by Illinois Governor John Peter Altgeld due to concerns about the fairness of the trial (Green 2006).

The Haymarket Incident had a lasting impact on the labor movement, setting back efforts to secure labor reforms in the short term. However, it also helped galvanize the labor movement globally, and May 1st, or May Day, became an International Day of Labor solidarity and remembrance (Smith 2016) (Figure 1.2).

Eight hours for work, eight hours for rest, and eight hours for what we will.

—Robert Owen

Figure 1.2 Hay Market incident of 1886

The Pullman Strike of 1894

The Pullman Strike of 1894 was a pivotal event in U.S. labor history, marked by significant economic disruption and violent clashes. It began on May 11, 1894, when workers at the Pullman Company, which manufactured luxury railroad cars in Chicago, went on strike in response to wage cuts, high rent in company-owned housing, and overall poor working conditions (Lindsey 2019). Despite reduced wages, the Pullman Company did not lower rent in its company-owned housing, which exacerbated workers' frustrations.

The strike gained momentum when the American Railway Union (ARU), led by Eugene V. Debs, supported the Pullman workers and organized a nationwide boycott of all trains using Pullman cars (Klein 2016). This boycott disrupted rail traffic and mail delivery across the country, causing widespread economic and logistical chaos. Over 125,000 workers were involved, leading to a virtual paralysis of the nation's rail system (Lindsey 2019).

In response to the disruption, President Grover Cleveland's administration sent federal troops to Chicago to break the strike, citing the interruption of mail services and interstate commerce as justification for

Figure 1.3 Pullman Strike of 1894

the intervention. Violent confrontations between the strikers and federal troops ensued, leading to multiple deaths and significant property damage (Klein 2016). The strike was ultimately crushed, and Eugene V. Debs was imprisoned for defying a federal injunction.

The Pullman Strike revealed deep-seated tensions between labor and management and underscored the federal government's willingness to intervene on behalf of business interests. However, this heavy-handed response strained the relationship between labor and the Cleveland administration. Recognizing the need to repair this relationship, President Cleveland signed legislation establishing Labor Day as a national holiday in 1894 (Lindsey 2019). While the government's intervention largely favored business interests, the severity of the strike's impact ultimately prompted federal leaders to reconsider labor rights (Figure 1.3).

The Establishment of Labor Day

Despite ongoing obstacles, American unions continued to achieve significant victories, including the establishment of Labor Day. Labor Day was

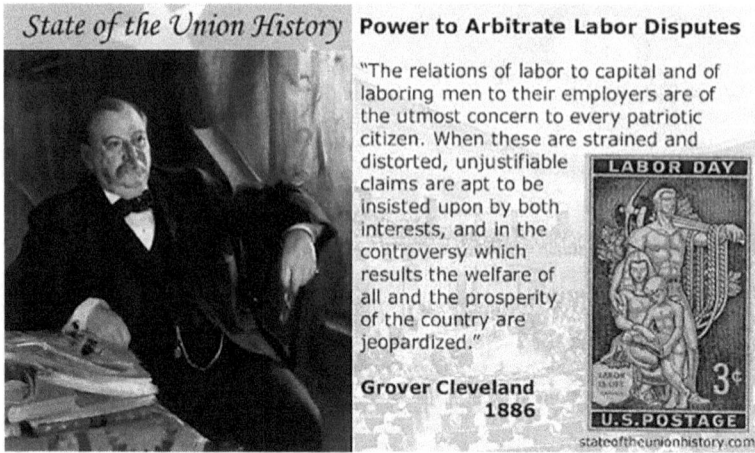

Figure 1.4 Power to arbitrate labor disputes—Grover Cleveland

first recognized by Oregon on February 21, 1887, as a national holiday (U.S. Department of Labor n.d.) (Figure 1.4).

Building on these early achievements, labor's influence continued to grow, prompting political leaders to respond with actions that recognized and supported workers' rights. This political engagement set the stage for significant milestones, such as Grover Cleveland's advocacy for labor reform and his eventual proclamation of Labor Day as a national holiday.

On June 28, 1894, during President Grover Cleveland's second term, he officially designated the first Monday of September as Labor Day. However, the origins of this move trace back a decade earlier to Cleveland's first campaign when he sought the support of the labor movement. Within his first 2 years in office, he advocated for expanding the Bureau of Labor's authority to mediate labor disputes. This may have been an attempt to prevent conflicts like the 1894 Pullman Strike, which occurred in the same year that Cleveland signed the proclamation creating the Labor Day holiday.

Cleveland's efforts to recognize labor's contributions were complemented by later significant legislation, such as the National Labor Relations Act (Wagner Act) of 1935, which strengthened workers' rights to unionize and bargain collectively (State of the Union History 2017).

The National Labor Relations Act

On July 5, 1935, Congress enacted the National Labor Relations Act (NLRA), establishing a clear policy to support collective bargaining by safeguarding workers' rights to freely associate. The NLRA ensures workplace democracy by granting employees in private sector workplaces the essential right to pursue improved working conditions and representation without fear of retaliation (National Labor Relations Board n.d.).

Often referred to as the *Wagner Act* in recognition of its drafter, New York Senator Robert F. Wagner, the law created a new national labor policy that has become one of the most enduring legacies of the New Deal. It established the right of employees to organize, form labor unions, and collectively bargain with their employers (Constitutional Law Reporter n.d.). The NLRA laid the foundation for modern labor relations, influencing contemporary workplace policies and union strategies (Figure 1.5).

Global Influence of Unions

Unions in the United States influenced labor movements worldwide. In Britain, the Trade Union Congress (TUC), established in 1868, unified trade unions to coordinate labor efforts. In continental Europe, industrialization spurred similar movements. The International Workingmen's Association (IWA), founded in 1864, sought to unite workers across nations to promote labor rights (Encyclopedia Britannica n.d.). Karl Marx

Figure 1.5 National Labor Relations Act—Roosevelt

played a significant role in shaping the IWA's ideology, emphasizing the importance of class struggle and workers' control over the means of production. Marx believed that "the working class would have to take political power and dismantle the capitalist system through revolution" (Marx 1976). The IWA actively supported various workers' movements, including the Paris Commune of 1871, a brief socialist government in Paris (Marxists Internet Archive n.d.).

However, ideological divisions within the IWA, particularly between Marxists and anarchists, contributed to internal conflict. Mikhail Bakunin, a prominent anarchist, disagreed with Marx's emphasis on centralization and state control, leading to significant tensions within the organization. These divisions eventually resulted in the dissolution of the IWA in the 1870s (Marxists Internet Archive n.d.). Despite its short existence, the IWA significantly influenced the international labor movement and laid the foundation for later organizations that advocated for workers' rights. These early transnational labor efforts underscored the universal challenges workers faced and demonstrated the need for international labor solidarity, which continues to influence contemporary labor movements and multinational labor policies.

The Role of Unions in Modern Workplaces

In today's rapidly evolving economic landscape, unions continue to play a crucial role in shaping workplace dynamics, advocating for fair wages, job security, and safe working conditions. While the labor movement has seen significant changes over the decades, unions remain a powerful force in ensuring that workers' rights are upheld in industries ranging from manufacturing to education and healthcare (Freeman and Medoff 1984). Their role extends beyond traditional collective bargaining; unions are now pivotal in addressing modern challenges such as technological disruption, globalization, and the rise of the gig economy (De Stefano 2016). As industries evolved, labor challenges also changed, requiring unions to adapt to new employment structures like the gig economy. While unions have traditionally protected full-time workers in established industries, a new challenge has emerged: the gig economy.

The gig economy, characterized by short-term contracts, freelance work, and on-demand employment facilitated through digital platforms, has transformed traditional employment models. Companies like Uber, DoorDash, and TaskRabbit exemplify this shift, where workers often forgo stable employment relationships in favor of flexibility. However, this new economic model frequently lacks the benefits, job security, and labor protections typically associated with traditional employment (De Stefano 2016). Unions are increasingly stepping into this space, advocating for gig workers by pushing for better pay, access to benefits, and legal recognition of their employment status.

By fostering collaboration between employees and management, unions contribute to the creation of equitable, productive, and sustainable work environments that benefit both workers and employers (Katz 2016). Understanding how unions operate and adapt is crucial for labor relations professionals, HR managers, and business leaders navigating today's workforce dynamics. This section explores the various facets of unions in the modern workplace, providing a comprehensive overview of their role and significance.

The Structure of Unions

Unions are typically organized into local, national, and international levels. Local unions represent workers within a specific geographic area or at a particular company. They are the grassroots organizations where individual workers are most directly involved. Local unions handle day-to-day issues, including grievances and workplace disputes. They are governed by elected officials who represent the interests of their members in negotiations with management (Friedman 2019).

National unions are larger entities that encompass multiple local unions. They provide broader support, resources, and strategic direction. National unions often engage in lobbying efforts to influence labor legislation and public policy. They also coordinate large-scale collective bargaining efforts and offer legal assistance to local unions. Examples of national unions include the United Auto Workers (UAW) and the American Federation of Teachers (AFT) (Friedman 2019).

International unions extend their reach across national borders, representing workers in multiple countries. These unions address global labor issues and advocate for international labor standards. They play a crucial role in industries where multinational corporations operate, ensuring that workers' rights are upheld regardless of geographic location. The International Trade Union Confederation (ITUC) is an example of an international union that promotes workers' rights worldwide (Baccaro 2017).

The Functions of Unions

The primary function of unions is to negotiate collective bargaining agreements (CBAs). These agreements set the terms and conditions of employment, including wages, benefits, working hours, and safety standards. CBAs are legally binding contracts that provide a clear framework for both employers and employees. They are renegotiated periodically to adapt to changing economic conditions and workplace needs (Katz 2016).

In addition to negotiating CBAs, unions play a vital role in grievance handling and dispute resolution. When employees face issues such as unfair treatment, unsafe working conditions, or violations of the CBA, the union steps in to represent their interests. This process often involves mediation and arbitration to resolve conflicts without resorting to strikes or legal action (Katz 2016). The grievance process typically involves multiple steps, each aimed at resolving the issue at the lowest possible level before escalating to more formal or external resolutions. While the exact steps can vary based on the CBA between the union and the employer, a typical grievance process includes the following steps:

1. **Informal Discussion**: In many cases, the grievance process begins with an informal discussion between the employee, their union steward, and their immediate supervisor. The goal at this stage is to resolve the issue quickly and amicably, without the need for formal documentation. This is often seen as a preventative measure to stop minor issues from escalating.
2. **Formal Written Grievance**: If the issue is not resolved informally, the next step is for the union or employee to submit a formal written grievance. This document outlines the specific complaint, citing

relevant sections of the CBA that are believed to have been violated. It is submitted to the employee's supervisor or the management representative designated to handle grievances.

3. **Management Review**: The grievance is reviewed by higher levels of management. This often involves meetings between union representatives and management to discuss the details of the grievance. At this stage, both sides may present evidence or arguments to support their position. Management then makes a decision on whether to uphold, modify, or deny the grievance.

4. **Appeal to Higher-Level Management**: If the grievance remains unresolved, it may be appealed to a higher level of management. At this stage, company executives or human resources personnel may become involved. Further meetings between union representatives and management occur to try to resolve the issue.

5. **Arbitration**: If the grievance is still not resolved after the internal steps, it may proceed to arbitration. Arbitration involves a neutral third-party arbitrator who reviews the case and issues a binding decision. Both the union and management present their evidence and arguments to the arbitrator, who then makes a final ruling.

These steps are intended to ensure that both the union and the management have adequate opportunities to resolve disputes internally before involving external parties. Each step is typically governed by specific timelines set out in the CBA to ensure timely resolution (Ithaca, NY: ILR Press, 2017).

Unions also engage in advocacy and political action. They lobby for labor-friendly legislation, support political candidates who prioritize workers' rights, and mobilize their members to participate in the democratic process. This political engagement helps shape policies that protect workers and promote fair labor practices (Friedman 2019).

Another critical function of unions is providing training and professional development. Many unions offer apprenticeship programs, continuing education, and skill enhancement opportunities to their members. These programs ensure that workers remain competitive in the job market and can adapt to technological advancements and industry changes (Baccaro 2017).

Benefits of Union Membership

Union membership offers numerous advantages for workers. Improved wages and benefits are among the most tangible benefits. Unionized workers typically earn higher wages than their nonunionized counterparts. They also receive better health insurance, retirement plans, and other benefits. These gains are a direct result of collective bargaining efforts that leverage the power of the collective to secure better terms for workers (Hirsch 2004).

Job security and protection from arbitrary dismissal are also significant benefits of union membership. Unions negotiate provisions that protect workers from being unfairly terminated. This includes requiring just cause for dismissal and ensuring due process in disciplinary actions. These protections provide a level of stability and peace of mind for workers, knowing that their employment is safeguarded by the CBA (Hirsch 2004).

Safer working conditions are another critical benefit. Unions advocate for stringent health and safety standards, ensuring that workplaces comply with regulations designed to protect workers. They also provide training and resources to help workers stay safe on the job. The presence of a union often leads to a more proactive approach to workplace safety, reducing the incidence of accidents and injuries (Katz 2016).

Unions also offer representation and support. In the event of a workplace dispute or grievance, union members have access to experienced representatives who can advocate on their behalf. This support is invaluable in navigating complex labor laws and employer policies. Union representatives bring expertise and resources that individual workers may lack, leveling the playing field in disputes with management (Friedman 2019).

Conclusion

The history of unions is a testament to the relentless pursuit of fairness and justice in the workplace. From their humble beginnings amid the harsh conditions of the Industrial Revolution to their significant role in contemporary labor relations, unions have profoundly influenced the dynamics between employers and employees. Their evolution reflects a journey marked by struggle, resilience, and triumph, illustrating the enduring power of collective action (Freeman and Medoff 1984).

Significant events such as the Haymarket Affair and the Pullman Strike highlighted the intense conflicts between labor and management and underscored the need for legal protections and formal recognition of unions. The establishment of key organizations like the National Labor Union in the United States and the TUC in Britain marked important milestones in the labor movement. These organizations laid the groundwork for modern unions by advocating for shorter workdays, better wages, and safer working conditions (Foner 1980).

Unions emerged as a response to the dire conditions faced by workers in the burgeoning industrial economies of the 18th and 19th centuries. The shift from agrarian economies to industrial powerhouses like the United States, Britain, Germany, and France not only brought about rapid economic growth but also led to widespread exploitation of labor. Workers, including children, endured long hours, unsafe environments, and inadequate wages. These challenging conditions prompted the formation of early unions, which sought to protect workers' rights and improve their working conditions (Epstein 1991).

One of the most notable achievements of unions was the successful fight for the 8-hour workday, a goal that was central to many labor movements around the world. The tragic events of the Haymarket Affair, where workers were killed during a rally for an 8-hour workday, galvanized support for labor reforms and highlighted the urgent need for improved working conditions. Such efforts culminated in the recognition of Labor Day as a national holiday in the United States, symbolizing the contributions and sacrifices of the labor movement (U.S. Department of Labor n.d.).

The passage of the NLRA in 1935 was a landmark moment in labor history. The NLRA provided legal protection for workers' rights to organize, form unions, and engage in collective bargaining. This legislation ensured that workers could pursue better working conditions and representation without fear of retaliation, fostering a more democratic and fairer workplace (Gross 1981).

Understanding the structure and functions of unions is crucial for anyone involved in labor relations. Unions operate at **local**, **national**, and **international** levels, each playing a distinct role in representing workers' interests. They negotiate CBAs, handle grievances, advocate for labor-friendly legislation, and provide training and professional development opportunities. Union membership offers numerous benefits, including improved wages and benefits, job security, safer working conditions, and access to representation and support in workplace disputes (Freeman and Medoff 1984).

Despite the significant achievements of unions, they continue to face challenges in the modern workplace. Declining membership, employer resistance, and the rise of the gig economy, all pose threats to traditional union models. However, unions must adapt to these changes by finding new ways to represent and advocate for workers, ensuring that they remain relevant and effective in a rapidly evolving labor market (Hirsch 2004).

As we move from exploring the historical foundations and the transformative role unions have played within the workforce, we enter a critical discussion that underpins much of labor management: the distinction between skilled and unskilled labor. Understanding this differentiation is not merely an exercise in classification, it is central to managing a unionized workforce effectively. The historical evolution of unions has been shaped by the collective power of both skilled and unskilled workers, each with unique needs, strengths, and expectations within the labor framework.

In Chapter 2, *Skilled and Unskilled Labor*, we delve into these categories, examining what defines each type of labor, how these roles are valued within industries, and how these distinctions influence workplace dynamics, labor relations, and management strategies. Recognizing the varied contributions of skilled and unskilled labor is essential for fostering respect, establishing appropriate expectations, and effectively negotiating within a unionized environment. Recognizing these distinctions is crucial for effective labor–management collaboration. In the next chapter, we explore how these labor categories influence workforce dynamics and management strategies.

CHAPTER 2

Skilled and Unskilled Labor: Definitions and Impacts

The skilled workers can stand on their own feet; they have the means of escape from the worst forms of exploitation. But the unskilled worker, driven from pillar to post, needs protection from every wind that blows. If labor is to be free, the unskilled worker must be organized.

—Samuel Gompers

This chapter is essential for **managers, supervisors, HR professionals**, and **union representatives** seeking to understand a core concept in workforce leadership: the critical distinction between skilled and unskilled labor. These terms are often used casually, yet their implications shape everything from workforce dynamics to contract negotiations, safety protocols, and training investments within unionized environments.

The quote by Samuel Gompers underscores the inherent differences between skilled and unskilled workers in terms of autonomy, bargaining power, and organizational needs. Gompers, a pioneering figure in the American labor movement and the first president of the American Federation of Labor (AFL), was a staunch advocate for workers' rights. He believed that unions should focus on tangible economic improvements and emphasized the importance of collective action in safeguarding the rights of vulnerable, unskilled laborers. Gompers' advocacy for labor rights underscores a key reality: While skilled workers often have leverage due to their expertise, unskilled workers historically depended on unionization to secure basic workplace protections and fair wages. This dynamic remains relevant in today's workforce management.

Defining Skilled Labor

Skilled labor forms the backbone of technical operations across nearly every major industry. These workers possess expertise developed through years of formal education, hands-on apprenticeships, certifications, or specialized vocational training. Roles such as electricians, welders, engineers, plumbers, machinists, and technicians exemplify this category, where precision, problem-solving, and applied knowledge are essential to daily operations.

Their contributions are far more than technical proficiency—they diagnose problems, make critical decisions, and ensure that complex systems function safely and efficiently. Their expertise comes at a premium, reflected in higher wages, union protections, and expectations for continuous learning. Skilled labor is, by its very nature, dynamic, evolving alongside the industries it serves.

Historically, skilled labor has also been at the forefront of technological innovation. Engineers pioneer new processes; IT specialists defend against cybersecurity threats; and electricians adopt smart grid technologies. Yet the rapid integration of AI is creating both opportunities and uncertainties for these professionals. Skilled labor now faces the dual responsibility of mastering their craft while adapting to AI-driven tools that augment their work.

While the characteristics of skilled labor are often discussed in terms of education, certifications, and technical expertise, the true essence of skilled work is perhaps best captured through its history and imagery. Skilled labor has long been associated not only with technical proficiency but also with courage, resilience, and a commitment to mastering complex tasks in demanding environments. One of the most powerful and enduring visual representations of this spirit can be found in the iconic 1932 photograph *Lunch atop a Skyscraper* (Figure 2.1).

The iconic image *Lunch atop a Skyscraper* not only captures a historical moment in the development of New York City's skyline but also embodies the essence of skilled labor during the early 20th century. The photograph, taken in 1932 by Charles C. Ebbets, depicts 11 ironworkers who were essential skilled laborers, precariously perched on a steel beam high above Manhattan during the construction of the RCA Building

Figure 2.1 Lunch atop a Skyscraper 1932

(now known as 30 Rockefeller Plaza). These men were part of the highly specialized workforce that contributed to the rapid urbanization and industrial growth of the United States during that period.

The image serves as a powerful representation of the skilled labor force, highlighting the combination of expertise, bravery, and resilience required to perform such dangerous work. Ironworkers, like those shown in the photograph, possessed specific skills in welding, riveting, and steel assembly, which were crucial in the construction of skyscrapers that defined the New York City skyline. The lack of safety equipment and the extreme heights at which they worked underscore the risk and physical demands placed on these workers, making the image a testament to the vital role that skilled labor played in shaping modern urban environments.

Furthermore, the photograph can be seen as a visual representation of the broader history and impact of skilled labor unions, which were instrumental in advocating for better working conditions, wages, and safety measures for workers in these demanding professions. The bravery and camaraderie depicted in *Lunch atop a Skyscraper* echo the values that skilled labor unions have long fought to protect.

Defining Unskilled Labor

Unskilled labor, though sometimes undervalued in societal discussions, is the essential infrastructure of daily operations in countless industries. These roles, often categorized by manual, repetitive tasks, include assembly-line workers, janitors, agricultural workers, warehouse associates, and general laborers.

Unlike skilled positions, unskilled labor requires little formal education or certification. However, the term "unskilled" should never be confused with "unimportant." The success of factories, warehouses, construction sites, and service industries depends on this workforce. Their contribution is vital—they maintain operations, ensure cleanliness and safety, and perform tasks fundamental to organizational efficiency.

Historically, unskilled labor has been especially susceptible to exploitation, often marked by lower wages, high turnover rates, and limited opportunities for advancement. These systemic challenges have made union advocacy indispensable. For decades, unions have played a critical role in championing the rights of unskilled workers—securing fair wages, improving safety standards, and demanding equitable treatment across industries.

To fully appreciate the historical role of unskilled labor, one must revisit one of the most transformative moments in American industrial history—the rise of mass production. Few innovations have shaped the landscape of unskilled labor more profoundly than Henry Ford's introduction of the moving assembly line. This breakthrough not only revolutionized manufacturing but also redefined the expectations, challenges, and opportunities for unskilled workers. The following image, taken in 1913 at Ford's Highland Park Plant, vividly captures this turning point—a visual representation of the early-20th-century workforce that powered industrial America. This image, set against the backdrop of Henry Ford's revolutionary introduction of the moving assembly line, highlights the significant role of unskilled labor in the mass production era that transformed American industry and society (Figure 2.2).

In contrast to skilled labor that required specialized training and expertise, unskilled labor in this context involved repetitive tasks that could be performed with minimal training. The introduction of the assembly

Figure 2.2 Unskilled workers

line allowed Ford to employ large numbers of unskilled workers to perform specific, simple tasks, thereby significantly reducing the cost and time of manufacturing automobiles. This approach not only made automobiles more affordable for the average American but also contributed to the broader industrialization of the United States.

The photograph of the workers on the flywheel assembly line symbolizes the shift from skilled artisanal work to mass production, where efficiency and productivity were prioritized over craftsmanship. This shift had profound implications for the labor force, as it not only created opportunities for unskilled workers but also led to monotonous, repetitive work that offered little in the way of skill development or job satisfaction.

Moreover, the reliance on unskilled labor in such settings highlighted the growing divide between skilled and unskilled workers. While skilled laborers were often able to negotiate better wages and working conditions through unions, unskilled workers had less bargaining power, leading to lower wages and less job security. This division played a crucial role in shaping labor relations and the development of labor unions in the 20th century.

The Management Challenge:
Two Workforces, Two Approaches

Managing skilled and unskilled labor within a unionized environment demands versatility. It requires an acute understanding of what motivates, challenges, and retains each group.

Skilled labor responds to leadership that respects their expertise. Managers leading these teams must foster autonomy, provide growth opportunities, and create space for problem-solving. Micromanaging skilled professionals is counterproductive; instead, success lies in setting clear expectations, investing in continued training, and recognizing technical achievements.

In contrast, managing unskilled labor effectively hinges on communication, consistency, and support. These workers thrive in environments where expectations are clear, contributions are acknowledged, and advancement opportunities, however modest, are available. Retention improves when managers demonstrate genuine respect for these essential roles, provide safety training, and offer paths toward skill development.

Skilled Versus Unskilled Labor:
A Practical Comparison

The management of skilled versus unskilled labor demands distinct approaches and highlights the value of tailored management techniques. Imagine a scenario where a manager with no technical background is placed in charge of a skilled workforce, such as electricians or welders. Although adept at people management and armed with a business degree, this manager may struggle to provide the technical direction required in emergencies, potentially leading to safety risks or inefficiencies. In skilled labor environments, experience and technical understanding are often nonnegotiable components of effective leadership.

Conversely, transitioning an experienced manager from a skilled trades environment to a role managing unskilled labor in a retail setting could be a smoother shift. In this instance, the manager's analytical skills and experience in team dynamics could enhance the efficiency and morale of the team. These examples illustrate the value of domain-specific expertise in skilled labor management, underscoring the distinct skills necessary to navigate the complexities of unionized skilled labor environments successfully. As these two labor categories continue to evolve, a new force is rapidly reshaping the landscape for both—AI. The next section explores how AI is redefining roles, responsibilities, and workforce strategies within unionized environments.

The Growing Role of AI in Shaping Labor Dynamics

As organizations increasingly integrate advanced technologies into daily operations, managers must prepare for a new layer of complexity in workforce planning: AI. While AI introduces tools for productivity and precision, it also reshapes traditional roles and introduces fresh challenges to unionized environments. Its impact diverges sharply across labor classifications—augmenting skilled roles while automating many unskilled ones.

AI's Emerging Influence on Skilled and Unskilled Labor

AI is redefining the landscape of both skilled and unskilled labor—but in different ways.

For skilled workers, AI is often a tool of enhancement. Predictive maintenance, data analytics, and automated diagnostics enable faster decision making and improved accuracy. Yet this also means that future skilled workers must be as comfortable interpreting data as they are wielding tools. AI literacy is becoming as vital as technical proficiency.

Unskilled labor, however, faces a more precarious reality. Automation threatens to eliminate roles defined by repetitive, manual tasks. Self-checkout machines, warehouse robots, and automated cleaning devices already displace certain positions. Managers leading unskilled teams must anticipate these trends, advocating for retraining, developing new job pathways, and collaborating with unions to protect displaced workers.

This intersection of technology, labor, and management will shape the future of unionized workforces. Forward-thinking leaders must prepare not only for operational changes but also for the human impact of AI-driven disruption.

Conclusion

The distinction between skilled and unskilled labor is not simply a classification of tasks—it is a strategic framework for modern management. Skilled labor brings specialized expertise critical to innovation and safety. Unskilled labor provides the operational muscle that keeps industries running. Both are essential. Both deserve respect. And both require tailored leadership.

Managers operating in unionized environments must recognize these differences, understand the unique contributions of each group, and foster environments where both skilled and unskilled workers can thrive. As AI and automation reshape the workplace, managers who can lead with adaptability, empathy, and foresight will not only navigate change—they will lead it.

To further illustrate the distinctions between skilled and unskilled labor, the Table 2.1 provides a side-by-side comparison of key characteristics, roles, and management strategies associated with each group. This visual guide demonstrates the contrasting aspects of skilled and unskilled labor, emphasizing the unique contributions and needs of each in a unionized workforce. By understanding these differences, managers can develop more tailored approaches that support productivity, engagement, and overall workforce cohesion.

The rise of AI and automation introduces new complexities to these roles, demanding that managers lead with both strategic foresight and contextual awareness. To build on this understanding, the next chapter explores how these two labor categories—skilled and unskilled—evolved into powerful collective forces through unionization. By tracing the development of their respective unions, we uncover how their strategies diverged, how they shaped modern labor policy, and how their contributions continue to define equitable work environments today.

Table 2.1 Skilled versus unskilled labor comparison

Aspect	Skilled labor	Unskilled labor
Definition	Workers with specialized knowledge, training, and education	Workers with minimal or no specialized training or education
Examples	Electricians, plumbers, engineers, and technicians	Assembly-line workers, janitors, agricultural workers, and general laborers
Training Requirements	Requires formal education, apprenticeships, and certifications	Minimal formal training, often learn on the job
Educational Background	Often requires advanced degrees or specialized certifications	Typically requires a high school diploma or less
Tasks Performed	Complex, technical, and specialized tasks	Routine, manual, and repetitive tasks
Problem-Solving Ability	High, involves diagnosing and resolving complex issues	Low to moderate, focuses on following instructions
Wages	Higher due to specialized skills and training	Lower due to minimal skill requirements
Turnover Rate	Lower, with more stable employment	Higher, with more frequent job changes
Career Advancement	Opportunities for significant career growth and professional development	Limited opportunities for advancement, often static roles
Impact on Productivity	Directly contributes to innovation and efficiency	Supports overall productivity through essential tasks
Economic Contribution	Significant, driving technological advancements and economic growth	Essential for maintaining daily operations and stability
Continuous Learning	Engages in ongoing education and professional development	Basic training with less emphasis on continuous learning
Examples of Training Programs	Apprenticeships, technical courses, and professional certifications	On-the-job training, basic safety and skills training
Role in Organizations	Often leads projects, develops new methods, and improves processes	Performs foundational tasks that support skilled workers and overall operations

CHAPTER 3

The History and Impact of Unionized Skilled and Unskilled Labor

This chapter is essential for *managers*, *HR professionals*, *union stewards*, and *business leaders* seeking to understand how unionized skilled and unskilled labor emerged and evolved over time. By examining their historical development and distinct paths to collective power, we gain a deeper understanding of labor–management dynamics and why certain labor strategies and union structures exist today.

Understanding the history of both skilled and unskilled labor is imperative to effectively managing unionized workforces. Labor unions, representing workers across a spectrum of trades and industries, have a rich and multifaceted history that has profoundly shaped the landscape of labor rights, workplace standards, and economic progress. These unions, whether advocating for highly skilled trades such as electricians and machinists or for unskilled workers in industries like manufacturing and service, have been instrumental in securing fair wages, safe working conditions, and equitable labor practices. To grasp their full impact and manage unionized workforces effectively, it is essential to explore the origins, evolution, and significant contributions of both skilled and unskilled labor unions. This historical context provides the foundation for effective leadership and informed decision making in environments where unionized labor is pivotal.

Divergent Paths: Skilled and Unskilled Unionization

Skilled labor unions typically followed the path of craft unionism, which was exclusive, trade-specific, and tightly regulated. The American

Federation of Labor (AFL), founded in 1886 by Samuel Gompers, exemplified this model. Focused on "pure and simple unionism," the AFL prioritized economic gains over political ideologies, emphasizing collective bargaining and the unique leverage of skilled workers in negotiation.

In contrast, industrial unionism took root among unskilled and semiskilled workers. Groups like the Congress of Industrial Organizations (CIO), established in the 1930s, united all workers within an industry regardless of skill level. Their strength came from numbers and solidarity. Industries such as steel, automotive, and mining, where vast labor pools were essential to operations, became strongholds for industrial unions.

This division between craft and industrial unionism was not just organizational; it reflected differing worldviews. Craft unions sought to limit access to trades to preserve wage strength and status. Industrial unions pushed for inclusivity, aiming to elevate large swaths of workers who had historically been excluded from both union protections and stable employment. While occasionally at odds, both models contributed significantly to worker protections, wage growth, and national labor policy.

Historical Milestones in Union Power

The skilled trades shaped union structure through rigorous apprenticeships, certifications, and safety standards. For example, the United Brotherhood of Carpenters and Joiners of America was instrumental in formalizing training and wage classifications in construction. Meanwhile, industrial unions drove key legislative wins such as the National Labor Relations Act (NLRA) of 1935, which guaranteed workers the right to organize, bargain collectively, and engage in concerted activity without employer retaliation.

Pivotal events like the Homestead Strike in 1892, the Pullman Strike in 1894, and the rise of CBAs throughout the 20th century underscore how skilled and unskilled unions shaped modern labor relations. Skilled workers often led the charge in securing formal agreements with detailed provisions, while industrial unions mobilized large-scale strikes and negotiations to shift public policy and employer behavior.

The Monongah Mining Disaster:
Catalyst for Safety Reform

One of the most significant impacts of labor unions has been their role in improving workplace safety. Historically, many industries had appalling safety records, with workers frequently exposed to hazardous conditions. Skilled labor unions were at the forefront of advocating for safer working environments, pushing for the implementation of safety regulations and standards. For example, the United Mine Workers of America (UMWA) played a critical role in securing better safety standards for miners, leading to a significant reduction in workplace accidents and fatalities (Derickson 1988).

The largest mining disaster in U.S. history that predates the formation of the UMWA occurred on December 6, 1907, at the Monongah Mine in Monongah, West Virginia. This catastrophic event, known as the Monongah mining disaster, resulted in the deaths of at least 362 miners, though some estimates suggest the number could be higher due to the inclusion of unregistered workers (McAteer 2007) (Figure 3.1).

The Monongah disaster is considered the worst mining disaster in American history and served as a significant catalyst for reform in mining

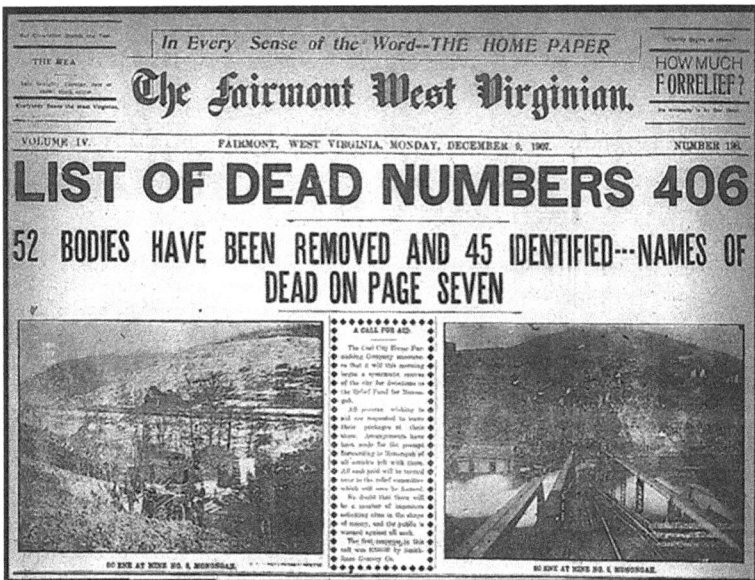

Figure 3.1 United Mine Workers of America—Mining disaster

safety regulations. It occurred before the UMWA was formed in 1890, but the incident underscores the hazardous conditions that miners faced, which the UMWA would later work to address.

The tragedy highlighted the dire need for better safety standards and labor representation in the mining industry, eventually contributing to the strengthening of labor movements, including the efforts of the UMWA to improve working conditions for miners across the United States.

In addition to safety improvements, skilled labor unions have also been instrumental in establishing apprenticeship and training programs. These programs ensure that workers acquire the necessary skills and knowledge to perform their jobs competently and safely. The apprenticeship model, which combines on-the-job training with classroom instruction, has been particularly successful in producing highly skilled tradespeople who meet industry standards (Bilginsoy 2003). While workplace safety remains one of unions' most enduring contributions, their impact extends beyond the shop floor. Economic stability, wage negotiations, and broader financial security for workers have been at the heart of union advocacy for over a century.

Economic Impact and Wage Negotiations

Labor unions have had a profound economic impact by negotiating higher wages and better benefits for their members, significantly shaping the labor market and broader economic trends. Through the process of collective bargaining, unions have been able to secure wage increases that not only keep pace with, but often exceed, inflation rates. This has ensured that workers' real wages—adjusted for the cost of living—do not stagnate, thereby preserving or even enhancing their purchasing power over time. The success of unions in these negotiations has a cascading effect on the broader economy. Higher wages among unionized workers lead to increased consumer spending, which is a critical driver of economic growth. When workers have more disposable income, they tend to spend more on goods and services, thereby stimulating demand and encouraging business investment and job creation (Freeman and Medoff 1984).

Moreover, the economic influence of labor unions extends beyond just the workers they represent. By setting a standard for wages and benefits within an industry, unions indirectly influence the pay and working conditions of nonunionized workers as well. This phenomenon, often referred to as the "union wage premium," benefits a broader segment of the workforce by raising the overall wage floor. Employers in nonunionized sectors may increase wages to remain competitive in attracting and retaining skilled labor, leading to wider economic benefits. Additionally, unionized industries often set benchmarks for labor practices, pushing industries nationwide to adopt higher standards for worker compensation and benefits, further contributing to economic stability and growth (Card 2001).

Furthermore, skilled labor unions have played a crucial role in addressing and mitigating income inequality. The advocacy for fair wages and comprehensive benefits packages helps to narrow the income gap between higher and lower earners within an industry. This has been particularly impactful in industries where skilled labor is essential but often undervalued or undercompensated. By fighting for equitable compensation, unions help to ensure that the economic gains of an industry are more evenly distributed among its workforce, rather than being disproportionately concentrated at the top. This redistribution of income not only promotes social equity but also supports economic stability by fostering a stronger middle class, which is vital for sustained economic growth (Card 2001).

In addition to wage negotiations, unions have also been instrumental in securing other economic benefits for their members, such as health insurance, pensions, and paid leave. These benefits, often achieved through CBAs, provide economic security to workers and their families, further enhancing their quality of life and reducing the financial strain associated with illness, retirement, or unexpected life events. The broader economic impact of these benefits is significant, as they contribute to a healthier, more productive workforce and reduce the social costs associated with poverty and inequality (Freeman and Medoff 1984).

The ripple effects of union-negotiated wages and benefits can also be seen in the broader community. Unionized workers tend to have more stable employment, higher incomes, and better benefits, all of which contribute to stronger, more resilient local economies. Communities with a strong union presence often enjoy higher standards of living, better public services, and more robust economic development. This is because the economic stability provided by union jobs translates into more consistent consumer spending, greater tax revenues, and a higher demand for goods and services within the community (Rosenfeld 2014).

Overall, the economic impact of labor unions through wage negotiations and collective bargaining has been profound, shaping not only the lives of the workers they represent but also the broader economy and society. By advocating for fair compensation and benefits, unions have played a critical role in promoting economic justice and ensuring that the gains of economic growth are more broadly shared.

Social and Political Influence

Beyond their economic contributions, labor unions have also had a significant social and political impact. Unions have been active in advocating for broader social justice issues, such as civil rights, gender equality, and immigrant rights. They have supported legislation that benefits all workers, not just their members, and have played a key role in shaping labor laws and regulations (Moody 1988).

Politically, labor unions have been powerful advocates for workers' rights, often aligning themselves with progressive movements and political parties. They have mobilized their members to vote, participate in protests, and support labor-friendly candidates. This political activism has helped to secure important legislative victories, such as the passage of the NLRA in 1935, which provided legal protections for union activities and collective bargaining (Gross 1981).

Relevance in the AI Era

Understanding this historical divergence is critical as we enter an era of rapid technological disruption. Skilled labor is adapting to AI-driven diagnostic tools and predictive analytics, while unskilled labor faces job displacement from automation and robotics. The future of unions may depend on how they integrate technological literacy, retraining programs, and equitable strategies across both labor segments.

Unions representing electricians and machinists may focus on upskilling members to work alongside intelligent systems. Industrial unions must advocate for broader protections, retraining, and job transitions for displaced workers. The legacies of craft and industrial unionism offer valuable insights into how unions might respond to the shifting demands of the 21st-century workforce (Acemoglu and Restrepo 2018).

Conclusion

The history of unionized skilled and unskilled labor is a story of parallel struggles, shared victories, and divergent strategies. From guilds to gig work, unions have evolved to meet the challenges of their time. By understanding how skilled trades protected their domain through exclusivity and certification and how unskilled labor leveraged solidarity to secure rights and representation, today's managers and union leaders can foster more effective collaboration.

Economically, unions have been pivotal in securing higher wages and better benefits for their members, contributing to a more equitable distribution of wealth and reducing income inequality. Through effective wage negotiations and the implementation of CBAs, unions have helped maintain workers' purchasing power and stimulated broader economic growth (Card 2001; Freeman and Medoff 1984).

Moreover, the social and political influence of unions extends beyond their immediate economic impact. They have been steadfast advocates for broader social justice issues and have significantly contributed to the advancement of civil rights, gender equality, and immigrant rights. Politically, their activism has shaped labor laws and ensured the protection of workers' rights, culminating in landmark legislation like the NLRA (Gross 1981; Moody 1988). While this chapter introduces the foundational economic and social influence of unions, Chapter 12 will explore these impacts in greater depth, focusing on their role in shaping equitable labor practices, societal structures, and the evolving American workforce.

As the 21st century progresses, a new era in labor history is emerging—characterized by advancements in AI, automation, and digital transformation. How unions respond to these forces will shape the next era of labor relations. Understanding their historical foundations and core distinctions is essential for managers tasked with balancing innovation, workforce development, and equitable representation in the digital age.

The next chapter begins a series of case studies drawn directly from my personal leadership journey managing unionized workforces across multiple sectors, including manufacturing, utilities, and power generation. These firsthand experiences highlight the practical challenges and successes that shaped my approach to labor relations. Through these real-world examples, we will explore actionable strategies for managing skilled and unskilled labor with clarity, confidence, and mutual respect.

PART 2

Personal Journey in Managing Unionized Workforces

CHAPTER 4

Navigating My First Supervisory Role with Unionized Labor

This chapter provides essential insights for *first-time supervisors* managing unionized workforces, **HR professionals** navigating labor relations, and *business leaders* working within unionized environments. While my experiences are rooted in skilled labor supervision, these lessons apply broadly across industries where CBAs govern workplace interactions.

Moving from a nonunion setting to a supervisory role in a unionized environment was both challenging and enlightening. Overseeing a team of skilled unionized workers in Upstate New York at 28, I quickly learned that the union culture required a different approach from which I was accustomed. My early confidence soon gave way to a deep respect for the traditions and expectations of unionized skilled labor. The following chapter explores the experiences that taught me valuable lessons in leadership, empathy, and collaboration, ultimately shaping my approach to managing union members.

Transition to Supervising Unionized Skilled and Unskilled Labor

My first supervisory job in Upstate New York involved overseeing a team of 7 to 20 employees. Before this role, I had worked with skilled trades (nonunion) for about 7 years. Managers new to unionized environments must quickly adjust their leadership approach to balance operational needs with contractual obligations. Unlike nonunion settings, where decisions may be more unilateral, unionized environments require collaboration with union stewards, adherence to seniority-based job assignments, and an understanding of structured grievance procedures.

At 28 years old, with no prior union experience, I transitioned into supervising unionized skilled labor. Coming from the Southern United States, where union presence was minimal, this brought about a significant shift. I had to quickly adapt to an environment that had deeply ingrained union traditions, regulations, and procedures. During my interview, when asked about my experience with unions, I admitted I had none. However, I mentioned that my father had been a Bargaining Chairman for the UAW (United Auto Workers; General Motors) and would help me get acclimated with the contract. In retrospect, thinking my father's guidance would suffice was naive—I had much to learn beyond just understanding and abiding by the contract.

In the early days of my transition, I found myself overwhelmed by the many nuances involved in managing unionized labor. From understanding the CBAs to navigating the complex relationships between union members, I realized there was a stark difference between the theoretical knowledge I had from observing my father and the real-world experience of handling union issues on the ground. My responsibilities extended beyond simply ensuring work was done; I had to understand the culture, the history, and the motivations behind union demands. The role required more empathy, patience, and a strategic approach than I had ever anticipated.

After a series of interviews, I secured the position of maintenance supervisor at Company A, overseeing employees from three unions: International Association of Machinists and Aerospace Workers (IAM); Bakery, Confectionery, Tobacco Workers and Grain Millers International Union (BCTGM, also known as BCT); and International Union of Operating Engineers (IUOE). Managing multiple unions presented unique challenges, including jurisdictional disputes, contract interpretation differences, and the necessity of balancing between diverse union priorities and ensuring operational efficiency.

Company A was a production facility that mass-produced, packaged, and shipped dog biscuits. The process was nearly fully automated with PLCs (programmable logic controllers), robots, servo motors, SCADA (supervisory control and data acquisition) systems, and computers. So, very little was completed manually except for maintenance, changeovers, packing (loading machines and moving pallets), and some shipping functions (loading pallets onto trucks). During orientation, I was handed an 8.5″ × 11″ red paperback book containing the contracts for each union. I was instructed to take it home and study it thoroughly. At that time, I had no idea what I was getting into.

The contracts were filled with clauses, stipulations, and language that required careful interpretation. I remember spending countless hours at my kitchen table, trying to absorb every detail and cross-reference each article. The more I read, the more I realized that understanding the words on paper was only half the battle. The true challenge lay in applying these contracts practically, respecting the collective agreement while balancing the operational needs of the facility.

I learned that relationships with union members would be central to my success. Developing trust and credibility was paramount, and it was not something that could be achieved overnight. In my initial interactions, I was met with skepticism and resistance. After all, I was the new guy—a young supervisor without any union background—and I represented management, which inherently positioned me as an outsider in the eyes of many union members.

In those early months, I made it a point to be visible on the shop floor, engaging with workers, asking questions, and listening to their concerns. I knew that to earn their respect, I had to show them that I was there to understand their perspective, not just enforce rules. I made mistakes, plenty of them, but I treated each mistake as a learning opportunity. I quickly discovered that union members valued consistency and fairness above all else. If they saw that I was willing to admit when I was wrong and correct my approach, they began to see me as someone they could work with.

Navigating the dynamics between the three different unions was also a significant learning curve. Each union had its own culture, leadership, and expectations. The IAM members, for example, had a strong focus on protecting their technical skills and job security, while the IOUE was more concerned with issues related to safety and working conditions due to the nature of their work with boilers, natural fuel, and high- and low-pressure steam systems. The BCT members, on the other hand, were focused on wages, shift schedules, and ensuring that unskilled labor was not overlooked in negotiations.

One of the most difficult aspects was dealing with the overlapping jurisdictions between the unions. There were times when disputes arose about which union had the right to perform certain tasks. I had to mediate these disputes carefully, ensuring that I was not perceived as favoring one union over another. This required a deep understanding of the contracts and an ability to facilitate discussions that led to a fair resolution. It was during these moments that I truly began to appreciate the complexity of managing unionized labor. The solutions were rarely black and white; they required compromise, negotiation, and a willingness to look at the bigger picture.

I also had to adapt my leadership style. In my previous role with non-union skilled trades, I had been more directive. I could assign tasks, and workers would generally comply without question. However, in my new role, I had to adopt a more collaborative approach, especially with the union steward. Union workers had a sense of ownership over their work, and they expected to have a voice in decisions that affected their jobs. I learned to involve them in planning and problem-solving, which ultimately led to better outcomes and a more cohesive team. The journey was not without setbacks, but each setback taught me something invaluable about leadership, communication, and resilience.

Growing Up in a Union Household: My Father's Influence

My father grew up in the union, starting at General Motors at 18, as did his father and nearly every family member (grandfather, father, aunt, uncles, and stepfather). Family gatherings often centered around union business. I vividly remember the 1980s, visiting the United Auto Workers (UAW) Union Hall on Tonawanda Street in Riverside, NY. The office and meeting room, located above a credit union, were always bustling with men discussing work, benefits, voting, and contracts. As Bargaining Chairman, my father traveled extensively within the United States—long before the advent of Zoom or Microsoft Teams.

Despite the challenges, I enjoyed the perks of my father's position, such as vacations, theme parks, picnics, and union family gatherings.

These experiences shaped my understanding of union culture as being not just about work but also about community and support.

However, it was not always enjoyable. I recall seeing my father on the 5 o'clock news discussing potential plant closures. One particularly memorable incident involved union employees smashing the windows of foreign-made cars in a parking lot, chanting **"Buy American and save our jobs."** This was akin to working for Apple and using an Android phone or working for Coca-Cola and bringing Pepsi to work—an action that would undoubtedly raise eyebrows.

At the age of 29, in 1981, my father led negotiations for two Local Agreements with the Chevrolet Division of GM and was instrumental in successfully initiating several national demands with General Motors Corporation. At the time, there were two agreements—one local with the Division and one National with the Corporation. These agreements were reached in the 1980s, a difficult period marked by plant closures and concessionary contracts, driven predominantly by tough global competition. One of my father's most notable accomplishments was restricting General Motors from using union retirement funds to build plants overseas. Although the company won that argument initially, the union gained a definitive voice in the allocation of retirement money. This set the pattern for jointly controlled corporate advance funding for healthcare, educational reimbursement, sick leave pay, and layoff assistance (Sub Pay)—protections that are still in effect today.

My father also negotiated on a local level for the highest-paid unskilled job classification in the entire corporation. This was achieved by leveraging the threat of a **Five Day Letter**, a notification to GM that they had 5 days from the initial notice to settle or the workers would go on strike. Many of his own members were happy with the result but wary of the alternative. The threat of a strike is powerful—but only until you really do walk out. It was incredibly stressful, and they shook hands after midnight on that fifth day. Plant closures were happening throughout the country in the 1980s, so it was a "gutsy" move that required both determination and skill.

Transition to Management: Bridging Two Worlds

At 28 years old, I started my job as a maintenance supervisor with only my family's union stories as my background. I was excited yet hesitant to share my new role with my family. After all, I was now on the "other side," as one family member humorously referred to me as **"Management Scum."** Despite this, my family was proud and respected my position, understanding the challenges that lay ahead.

Growing up in a union household taught me that union members were not just employees—they were a community that looked out for one another, fought for their rights, and took pride in their work. This understanding was both a strength and a challenge as I transitioned into management. On one hand, it allowed me to empathize with the workers I was managing, understanding their sense of unity, their challenges, and their dedication to fairness and respect. This empathy was crucial in building trust with my team. It helped me demonstrate that, even as a member of management, I valued their contributions and understood the struggles they faced.

On the other hand, my new role required me to uphold company policies and make tough decisions that were not always popular with the workers. Balancing these responsibilities required me to learn how to negotiate effectively, communicate transparently, and make decisions that, while sometimes difficult, were in the best interest of both the workers and the organization. This balancing act was one of the most challenging aspects of my early management career, but it also provided the foundation for my growth as a leader.

Overview of the Unions I Supervised

My first experience supervising unionized employees was comprised of three different unions. Two of the three unions were skilled, and one was unskilled. The skilled unions were the IAM (International Association of Machinists and Aerospace Workers) and the IUOE (International Union of Operating Engineers), while the unskilled union was the BCTGM (Bakery, Confectionery, Tobacco Workers and Grain Millers International Union).

The International Association of Machinists and Aerospace Workers (IAM)

The International Association of Machinists and Aerospace Workers (IAM), also known as the IAM or simply machinists, is one of the largest and oldest labor unions in North America, representing a broad array of workers primarily in the manufacturing and aerospace sectors (International Association of Machinists and Aerospace Workers 2023). Founded on May 5, 1888, in Atlanta, Georgia, the union was originally established by 19 machinists who sought better wages, working conditions, and job security for skilled workers in the rapidly industrializing United States (Gould IV 2022). Over time, the IAM expanded to represent over 600,000 active and retired members across the United States and Canada, advocating for workers in industries including defense, transportation, aerospace, healthcare, and others.

One of the key strengths of the IAM is its ability to negotiate favorable contracts for its members. The union is recognized for securing strong CBAs, including wage increases, benefits such as healthcare and retirement plans, and protections against unfair labor practices. For example, as of 2023, the IAM has secured contracts with major companies such as Boeing, Lockheed Martin, and United Airlines, providing long-term stability and financial security for workers. The IAM is also an active participant in political advocacy, supporting legislation that protects workers' rights and promotes fair trade policies to protect jobs in the industries it represents.

The International Union of Operating Engineers (IUOE)

The IUOE is one of the most significant and well-established labor unions in North America, representing workers who operate and maintain heavy equipment used in construction, mining, utilities, and other sectors (International Union of Operating Engineers 2023). Founded in 1896, the IUOE has grown to represent over 400,000 members across the United States and Canada. Its members include operating engineers, who work with cranes, bulldozers, and other heavy machinery, as well as stationary engineers, who manage and maintain building systems like heating, ventilation, air conditioning, and power generation systems.

One of the defining features of the IUOE is its comprehensive apprenticeship and training programs. Through a network of more than 100 local unions, the IUOE operates state-of-the-art training facilities that provide members with the technical skills required to operate complex machinery safely and efficiently. This focus on skills development is crucial in an industry where technological advancements are continually reshaping the work landscape (IUOE National Training Fund 2022).

The Bakery, Confectionery, Tobacco Workers, and Grain Millers International Union (BCTGM)

The BCTGM, often referred to as BCT, represents workers in a wide range of food processing industries, including the production of baked goods, confectionery items, tobacco products, and grain milling (Bakery, Confectionery, Tobacco Workers, and Grain Millers International Union 2023). Founded in 1886, the union has evolved significantly over the years and now advocates for more than 70,000 members in the United States and Canada. BCTGM members work in companies that manufacture some of the most recognized brands in the world, such as Kellogg's, General Mills, Hershey's, and Mondelez International.

A hallmark of the BCTGM's efforts is its strong commitment to workers' rights through collective bargaining and organizing. The union has been at the forefront of advocating for better wages, pensions, health benefits, and protection from layoffs. One of the most notable examples of the union's power was the 2021 strike at Kellogg's plants, where BCTGM members protested against the company's proposed two-tiered wage system, which they argued would negatively affect newer employees. After months of negotiations and public attention, the workers secured a contract that maintained their benefits and provided for wage increases, underscoring the union's success in standing up for its members (Scheiber 2021).

Early Challenges and Learning Experiences

In an effort to make my personal story more relatable to my journey of learning things along the way, I present here a chronological timeline of my experiences and learnings. After all, I did not just read the contract and understand what was on paper versus what happened on the job. That being said, I want to describe what and how I learned things on the job starting out as a 28-year-old learning the ropes.

For example, I didn't know what a PERB (Public Employment Relations Board) charge was, what "blackballed" meant, that there were different steps in the grievance process, or that overtime polling was done differently at different companies/unions. Some unions couldn't strike, some unions were weak, and some were strong. Let me just tell my story organically, highlighting my trials and tribulations along the way.

My Journey at Company A

My journey started at Company A, which lasted approximately 10 years. I spent the first five years supervising skilled labor exclusively. Later, I was promoted to an operations supervisor role, where I managed both skilled and unskilled labor for the remaining 5 years. This dual responsibility marked the culmination of my career with Company A.

A Year of Trials and Lessons

In my first year, I underwent rigorous testing, akin to a hazing period, which made me appreciate the power of the union and, more importantly, the power of unionized skilled labor. One key piece of advice I offer is: "Never think you know everything when it comes to skilled labor." The moment you disregard their advice or exclude them from decision making, you jeopardize your success.

Initially, I was aggressive and somewhat bullheaded, believing I knew what was required for each job. After all, prior to becoming a supervisor, I was an industrial mechanic/electrician (nonunion); therefore, I had done some of the jobs of the people I was supervising. This approach backfired. My crew followed my orders without question, but this led to significant errors since my instructions were often incorrect as a 28-year-old supervisor/tradesman. I soon realized that I was undermining the expertise of skilled employees with decades of experience. Once I acknowledged my limitations and began seeking the advice of skilled workers, my job and relationships became much smoother. However, challenges persisted.

One night, during the second shift (3–11:30 p.m.), a breakdown occurred, and with all electricians busy, I decided to troubleshoot a piece of equipment using an electrical meter. Within minutes, a 62-year-old electrician named Sam confronted me, furious that I had encroached on his job. He yelled at me, "What the hell are you doing? You don't touch tools; you are taking money out of our pockets!" At first, this scared me as if I were doing something unsafe; I was just trying to help get the machine up and running.

Later, I spoke with the electrician privately, not fully understanding my wrongdoing. Sam told me, "This is my job, not yours. You are a supervisor, not an electrician. You do not touch tools or do another person's job." I later learned that it applied to menial tasks such as sweeping up the floors, moving my computer, hooking up a printer, throwing out trash, and organizing the parts room. This incident led to my first grievance, requiring me to pay the highest senior electrician 4 hours of call-in pay because I had used a multimeter. Quickly and painfully, I understood Sam's actions and rationale.

I often wondered how Sam made it over to me so fast after I picked up the multimeter, as if he already knew what I was doing. I found out that an equipment operator recognized me working with a multimeter and called the shop steward, who then called Sam to confront me. This experience underscored the importance of respecting established roles and boundaries within union environments, a critical lesson in understanding union culture.

Understanding the Grievance Process

Let me circle back to the Step A grievance I received, which marked my first experience navigating the structured dispute resolution process. Step A is the initial stage in addressing labor disputes, requiring careful documentation and adherence to contractual obligations. For HR professionals and labor relations specialists, understanding grievance procedures is critical in maintaining fairness and preventing unnecessary escalation. Each step in the grievance process serves as a structured opportunity to address disputes, and how these are handled can significantly impact workplace morale and trust between management and employees.

Upon receiving the grievance, I documented it, signed it to acknowledge receipt, and provided a copy to the union steward. This step required meticulous attention to detail, as escalating a grievance could have significant implications for labor–management relations.

After reviewing the grievance with my manager, we determined that, per the contract, the highest-seniority first-shift electrician was entitled to 4 hours of call-in pay. As a result, the grievance was resolved at Step A and did not escalate to Step B.

Please note that I have been involved in all steps of the grievance process up to and including arbitration. Each grievance step is a process and takes time. In the end, the union must determine if they want the grievance to go in front of a judge/arbitrator. This process costs both the company and the union money, so arbitration is not taken lightly and doesn't happen often. The goal is for both the union and the management to sit down at a table and come to an agreement long before arbitration. After all, grievances take time, effort, and money, so the goal for both parties is to resolve them as soon as possible. In addition, the grievance process can harbor animosities, ill feelings, and trust issues. However, navigating it successfully helps build respect between management and union members.

Brotherhood and Loyalty Among Union Members

Another lesson learned was that Brothers and Sisters take care of each other, irrespective of union or trade. I remember a time, on third shift, when I walked through the main men's locker room. Walking through the locker room was almost taboo—an untold rule that supervisors did not go in the rank-and-file locker room; it was considered as their personal space. However, I was looking for someone because I had equipment down and needed support, and no one was picking up on the radio. For business leaders unfamiliar with union dynamics, it is important to recognize that unions function as tightknit communities built on mutual loyalty and shared advocacy. Attempting to implement change without considering these dynamics can result in resistance. A strategic approach that respects union solidarity while aligning with business goals is essential for long-term success.

The person I was looking for was tipped off by someone who saw me going into the locker room. Coincidentally, that person called me on my cellphone within a few minutes. I am not insinuating that the person was doing something wrong; I just could not locate him after numerous calls over the loudspeaker. That being said, I have the utmost respect for their unity and looking out for each other. The point I am trying to convey here is that this bond union members have is extremely strong and impenetrable. So, don't think for one moment you are going to do something you shouldn't, and a union member is going to turn a blind eye—you'll be sadly mistaken. However, if a union member does break that trust and speaks ill of another, he or she can be "blackballed"— another lesson learned.

Blackballed: What It Means

Being "blackballed" within a union setting refers to a practice where a worker is systematically excluded or ostracized from union activities or employment opportunities, often due to perceived disloyalty or conflict with union leadership. This term originally came from the use of a literal black ball in secret votes to reject new members. In the modern context, blackballing can occur when an individual's actions are seen as going against the collective interests of the union, such as crossing a picket line or supporting management during labor disputes (Heery and Noon 2017).

Blackballing can have significant repercussions on a worker's career, as unions play a critical role in employment opportunities, especially in industries with a strong union presence (Strauss 1991). The practice, although informal, can create a chilling effect on dissent within the union and can challenge democratic governance within labor organizations. Luckily, I have not been involved or observed any union members being blackballed in my 25 years, which says a lot about their union loyalty.

Managing Overtime Pay

A key challenge in my first year was managing overtime—a process closely overseen by both supervisors and union stewards. If there was overtime, I had a list of employees that I would have to go around and ask/poll. If it required an electrician, I had a pool of two or three of them on nightshift to ask, and if they didn't want the overtime, I could call in the most senior person from dayshift or the upcoming shift. Note, I could not call people who were on vacation or sick. If no one wanted the overtime, then I had to force the least senior electrician on the shift. For managers, ensuring that overtime distribution aligns with contractual obligations is critical in avoiding grievances and worker dissatisfaction. Union stewards play a vital role in monitoring this process to ensure fairness and compliance with seniority rules. Missteps in overtime allocation can quickly escalate into disputes, making transparency in scheduling essential.

A lesson I learned early on was not to skip anyone. As a new supervisor, I thought, "Hey, there's Tony—I'll ask him even though he's second on the overtime list." Tony said yes, and then I thought, "What if Bruce wants it; he's first on the list?" I crossed my fingers, hoping he would decline the overtime, but Bruce said yes. I was now stuck with two people when the overtime request was originally intended for one person.

Later, my boss asked why we paid two people for that job the previous night. I had to reply that I messed up and did not follow the enumerated seniority list. Additionally, when calling in people from the next shift, I had to have the union steward present to verify and witness that they were called and that I left a detailed message. We usually gave the person or persons called 30 minutes to call back before we considered it an automatic decline, and then we forced the lowest senior tradesman.

Building Credibility

My first year was a formative experience—learning through trial, error, and constructive feedback from the union members I supervised. Building credibility with union members requires understanding the boundaries set by contracts, the importance of consistent and fair treatment, and the value of seeking advice from experienced workers. This foundation set the tone for my approach to unionized environments, helping me transition from a directive leadership style to one that valued collaboration and mutual respect.

Conclusion

For first-time supervisors, this chapter highlights the importance of adaptability, communication, and mutual respect when leading a unionized workforce. HR professionals can take away key lessons on navigating grievances and fostering collaboration, while business leaders can use these insights to develop strategies that balance operational goals with labor relations best practices. Understanding union culture is not just about compliance; it is about creating a work environment that respects both management priorities and employee rights while fostering mutual trust and cooperation.

Reflecting on my first supervisory role managing unionized skilled and unskilled labor, I recognize how transformative this experience was. Moving from a nonunion environment to one with multiple unions required me to adjust quickly, build trust, and embrace the complexities of labor relations. I learned that effective management is not just about enforcing policies and ensuring operational efficiency. It demands patience, active listening, and a willingness to engage in meaningful dialogue with employees to address concerns while upholding company expectations.

These lessons shaped my leadership approach in ways I could not have anticipated at the start of my career. Initially, I approached my role with a directive mindset, assuming that authority alone would drive productivity. However, I quickly discovered that unionized environments function on deeply ingrained principles of fairness, transparency, and collective decision making. To succeed as a leader, I had to shift toward collaboration, recognizing that workers value consistency and respect above all else. When management approaches unionized labor with an open mind and a fair approach, conflicts become opportunities for problem-solving rather than barriers to progress.

Over time, I came to appreciate that leadership in a unionized setting is both an art and a science. It requires a careful balance between protecting the company's interests and ensuring that employees feel heard, valued, and respected. Developing credibility among union members was not an overnight process. Every decision, from grievance handling to shift scheduling, was closely observed and evaluated for fairness. By making transparency and integrity the foundation of my leadership style, I was able to build trust, foster cooperation, and strengthen labor–management relations in meaningful ways.

Looking back, my early mistakes in grievance handling, jurisdictional disputes, and overtime management were not just challenges but were also invaluable learning experiences. Each obstacle reinforced the importance of respecting contractual boundaries, engaging in open communication, and remaining flexible in the face of evolving labor dynamics.

True leadership in a unionized environment is not about asserting authority or rigidly adhering to company policies at the expense of worker concerns. It is about building trust, fostering collaboration, and ensuring that every interaction strengthens rather than erodes relationships between labor and management. As I progressed in my career, I realized that leadership is not defined by how many decisions I make but by how well I create an environment where employees feel empowered to contribute their best work.

Managing a unionized workforce requires more than just technical knowledge or a firm grasp of labor laws. It demands emotional intelligence, adaptability, and a commitment to fairness. By embracing these principles, managers and supervisors can turn potential challenges into opportunities to build stronger, more productive, and more cohesive teams.

CHAPTER 5

Insights from Managing Unions in a Foundry

Introduction to the USW and the Foundry Environment

My second union supervisor and manager role was in Niagara Falls, New York (Company B), where I worked with the United Steelworkers (USW). At Company B, the USW represented both skilled and unskilled workers. Skilled union members included electricians, welders, and millwrights, while unskilled workers operated heavy equipment such as cranes, large wheel loaders, forklifts, and skid steers. Before sharing my union challenges and experiences, it is best to provide some information about the USW.

The USW is one of the largest and most influential labor unions in North America, representing workers in a diverse range of industries, including steel, aluminum, oil, chemical, rubber, paper, and healthcare (United Steelworkers 2023). Founded in 1942, in the midst of World War II, the USW was initially created to protect the interests of workers in the steel industry, but it quickly expanded its membership to include workers in other sectors. Today, the USW boasts over 850,000 active members and retirees in the United States, Canada, and the Caribbean, making it one of the most powerful voices in labor (United Steelworkers 2023).

Throughout its history, the USW has been a strong advocate for workers' rights, securing better wages, working conditions, and benefits for its members. The union has a long track record of successful CBAs with some of the largest corporations in the industries it represents, including U.S. Steel, Alcoa, and Chevron. One of the key areas of focus for the USW has been workplace safety, especially in high-risk industries like steel and chemical production. The union has pushed for stricter safety regulations and implemented comprehensive health and safety training programs for its members, helping to reduce workplace accidents and fatalities (Bureau of Labor Statistics 2022).

In addition to its role in collective bargaining, the USW has been an active participant in political advocacy. The union has supported legislation promoting fair trade, workers' rights, and environmental protections. For instance, the USW has been a vocal advocate for Buy American policies, which seek to protect domestic manufacturing jobs from being outsourced to countries with lower labor standards. The USW also played a pivotal role in the passage of the United States–Mexico–Canada Agreement (USMCA), which replaced the North American Free Trade Agreement (NAFTA) and includes stronger labor protections for workers in all three countries (United Steelworkers 2023).

Transition to the Foundry: A Different World

I was hired for a hybrid position as a maintenance manager and electrical engineer at Company B, a foundry that presented an entirely different work environment than I had ever experienced. It was not only hot, dirty, and dangerous but also required a heightened awareness of safety and endurance. I mention this because, through my journey, I discovered that unions and workers are often tied to their specific working environments. My first position was at a food manufacturing facility, which was much cleaner compared to a foundry. In addition, the culture and the people were much different.

In a foundry, the furnace can reach up to 5,000 degrees Fahrenheit, and there are ladles of molten metal flying overhead. The workers in this environment faced physical challenges every day, including dealing with intense heat, and the physical endurance required to do their job without succumbing to heat exhaustion or being splashed with molten metal. For instance, to tap a furnace, you would fire an 8-gauge shotgun into the structure to get the molten metal flowing out of the tap hole. Employees had to wear cooling suits to avoid melting in front of the tap hole.

The environment was chaotic, and every day presented new challenges. Workers had to be vigilant, not just for their own safety, but also for the safety of their coworkers. The camaraderie and mutual dependence among workers were essential for survival in this extreme setting. Transitioning from a controlled food-grade facility to a volatile foundry filled with molten metal and extreme heat required a complete shift in both mindset and leadership approach. Interestingly, despite the USW's strong national presence, its influence at our foundry was relatively weak. At Company B, I was able to develop work schedules directly with employees, bypassing the formal involvement of the steward or union president. We simply sat together, discussed options, and implemented a mutually agreeable schedule without any issues. In contrast, at Company A—as well as at Companies C and D—such direct engagement would have been classified as direct dealing, a violation that could have led to a PERB (Public Employment Relations Board) charge. So, what is a PERB charge? I'm glad you asked.

Understanding PERB Charges

A PERB charge refers to a labor dispute complaint filed with the Public Employment Relations Board (PERB), which governs public sector employment disputes. While PERB handles cases involving state and municipal workers, the National Labor Relations Board (NLRB) serves a similar function for private sector employees. Understanding the distinction between these two bodies is essential for managers navigating labor relations across different industries (California Public Employment Relations Board 2023).

A PERB charge is usually filed when there is an allegation of an unfair labor practice (ULP) by either an employer or a union. Unfair labor practices might include:

Employer Actions
- Interfering with employees' rights to organize or join a union.
- Retaliating against employees for participating in union activities.
- Refusing to bargain in good faith with a union representing its employees (PERB 2023).

Union Actions
- Failing to represent union members fairly.
- Engaging in coercion of workers to join the union.
- Refusing to negotiate in good faith with the employer (PERB 2023).

In practical terms, a PERB charge can be filed by an employee, a union, or an employer who believes that the other party has violated provisions of state labor laws that govern public sector employment (California Public Employment Relations Board 2023). For example, if an employer unilaterally changes the working conditions without consulting the union, the union could file a PERB charge alleging a failure to bargain in good faith.

After a PERB charge is filed, the agency generally investigates the claim to determine if there is sufficient evidence of an ULP. If so, they may proceed with a hearing where evidence can be presented, and, ultimately, they may issue an order or directive to remedy the situation (California Public Employment Relations Board 2023).

PERB charges can be lengthy and arduous, often involving multiple hearings and appeals. The process is intended to ensure fairness but can be a heavy burden on both the union and the management. The key takeaway is that avoiding direct dealing or bypassing the union is critical to maintaining proper labor relations. This lesson became more apparent to me as I moved to other companies with stronger union presences.

Challenges and Unusual Experiences at Company B

Another example of the weak union presence at Company B was that I don't recall ever receiving any grievances, despite knowing that I didn't do everything by the book. One such instance was when I created a training program (Apprentice Training Document listed in Appendix K) for an employee who wanted to become an electrician. Typically, doing this without union involvement would be considered taboo and could lead to a PERB charge. However, it was not pursued, I worked with human resources, and they approved a 4-year program for the employee to move from an operator role to an electrician. Remarkably, that employee is now a certified journeyman electrician, which was eventually approved and endorsed by the USW Union. In addition to creating an apprenticeship program, I was able to make a radical change to the normally scheduled work week and hours. The change impacted all of the skilled trades in my department. This change was not made with the endorsement of the Union; it was simply that I noticed a need to revise the schedule to better adapt employees' lives and the companies' needs. I had given my employees a 1-month notice, and the schedule was implemented without a grievance.

The people in the organization were what I would describe as thick-skinned. The majority of workers were men, with only a handful of women working in production and none in skilled trades. This was not due to bias—it was simply a reality of the physical demands of the work. The foundry environment was extremely dangerous and tested workers' mental and physical fortitude. I remember standing in the furnace with a 67-year-old man named Fred, who was swinging a 10-pound sledge-hammer for what seemed like forever. I suggested, "Hey Fred, why don't you take a break and let me take a couple of swings at that bellows." He stopped, straightened up, looked at me, and said, "No," while laughing. His response was clear: "Don't insult me!"

Fred represented the spirit of the foundry worker—pride, resilience, and an unbreakable will. The foundry workforce shared a deep sense of loyalty and commitment. They worked in extreme conditions, and there was a sense of toughness that was palpable. At Company B, as a manager, I could actually work alongside the team, although technically it wasn't allowed. However, in a hot furnace filled with carbon monoxide after a recent shutdown, workers took all the help they could get. I had my first experience with an arc torch cutting stainless steel, racking out 13.8KV breakers (shown in the images below), welding, using an acetylene torch, and repairing overhead cranes. All this was possible because the union presence at this facility was not as strong as others. This is not to say the USW Union is weak; it is simply my experience in 2011 at Company B (United Steelworkers 2023) (Figures 5.1 and 5.2).

This flexibility allowed me to build relationships with my team. They respected my willingness to get my hands dirty and work alongside them. While this may have blurred the traditional lines between management

Figure 5.1 Nick E. Gilewski performing work with USW Electricians

Figure 5.2 Nick E. Gilewski in ARC Flash PPE

and labor, it forged a bond that was crucial for our success. It was a balancing act—being part of the crew when needed but still maintaining authority as a supervisor.

Remembering Fred

I would be remiss not to mention Fred again. About a year later, Fred tragically passed away. While at work, I received an emergency call that Fred had fallen and hit his head on the railroad tracks where they brought in coal. We called 911, and he was rushed to the hospital. Someone mentioned that he had felt dizzy and fallen onto the tracks, hitting his head.

At the hospital, Fred needed ten staples in his head. When asked if he wanted a shot to numb the pain, he replied, "No!" They had to remove and reinsert the staples later for an MRI, all without pain medication. This incident speaks to the type of person who works at a metal foundry—a testament to the work ethic and resilience it takes to endure that environment. Fred returned to work after his cancer diagnosis, retired shortly after, and sadly passed away a few months later.

Fred's story is a reflection of the commitment and sacrifice found in the industrial workforce. It is also a reminder of the human side of labor—these are individuals who dedicate their lives to dangerous and grueling work, often with little recognition. The bonds formed in such environments are unique, forged through shared hardship, and tested by the demands of the job. Fred's memory lived on among his colleagues, and his legacy was one of toughness and loyalty.

Company A was different in that things were more formal and "by the book." I constantly referred to the union contract, highlighting and earmarking sections to prepare for any disputes. I could recite sections if necessary. At Company B, I rarely referenced the contract. Overtime management was also different—Company B based it purely on seniority. If there was overtime, the most senior person was asked, and if they declined, the next in line was asked. Company A, by contrast, kept detailed records of overtime hours, ensuring everyone had an opportunity to work overtime. If no one volunteered, the lowest on the totem pole was forced. This approach effectively incentivized people to take overtime when it was available.

Conclusion

My 2 years at Company B were a profound learning experience that tested my adaptability, resilience, and leadership in ways I had not anticipated. The foundry environment was unlike anything I had previously encountered, requiring a shift in management approach to navigate both the extreme physical conditions and the unique union dynamics. The relatively weak union presence allowed for more direct interaction with employees, enabling me to build strong relationships and foster mutual respect between management and labor.

Working in such a demanding setting gave me invaluable insight into the daily challenges faced by foundry workers. I developed a deep appreciation for their endurance, dedication, and ability to perform under intense conditions, both physically and mentally. Managing a team in this environment reinforced a key leadership principle: True effectiveness is not just about enforcing policies but also about engaging directly with employees, listening to their concerns, and demonstrating respect for their expertise and the obstacles they overcome.

The camaraderie among workers at Company B was shaped by the extreme conditions they endured together. While the traditional lines between supervisor and employee were sometimes less rigid, the trust and cooperation we built contributed to a more cohesive and productive work environment. This experience reinforced the importance of adaptability in leadership. Recognizing the distinct characteristics of different workplaces and adjusting my approach accordingly were just as essential as maintaining structure and operational efficiency.

Fred's story stands as a powerful testament to the resilience, dedication, and unyielding spirit of industrial workers. His commitment to his craft and the strength he displayed in his final years embodied the very essence of the foundry workforce. Managing in a high-risk, physically demanding environment reinforced the need for supervisors to be both adaptable and actively engaged with their workforce. Leadership in these settings goes beyond enforcing policies; it requires understanding the workforce's daily struggles, recognizing their expertise, and earning their trust.

HR professionals can apply these insights to better balance structured labor relations with the realities of daily operations, while business leaders can draw lessons on fostering collaboration and communication in environments with varying union dynamics. Ultimately, my time at Company B was a formative chapter in my leadership journey. It reinforced the idea that effective management is not just about implementing policies but also about understanding the workers, respecting their expertise, and maintaining a workplace culture where safety, dignity, and labor–management cooperation remain at the forefront—regardless of industry or union strength.

CHAPTER 6

Transitioning to Power Generation with the IBEW

For *supervisors* stepping into unionized environments, *HR professionals* tasked with maintaining labor relations, and *business leaders* responsible for workforce management, this chapter provides a firsthand look into navigating one of the most influential trade unions in North America—the International Brotherhood of Electrical Workers (IBEW). For those tasked with leading in a unionized environment, few challenges are as revealing as managing a workforce through a contract impasse. At Company C, I encountered firsthand how labor disputes, workforce slowdowns, and contract negotiations shape both daily operations and long-term labor relations. The lessons in this chapter will equip you with the tools to manage union dynamics effectively—whether you are a frontline supervisor, an HR leader handling grievances, or an executive making strategic decisions about workforce engagement. Whether you are leading a unionized team, designing HR policies, or making strategic decisions about labor relations, the insights shared in this chapter will prepare you for the complexities of managing strong union dynamics while maintaining operational efficiency and workplace morale.

My third union supervisory role was at Company C in Niagara Falls, New York, where I managed a workforce represented by the IBEW. Despite the union's name, its members at Company C included both skilled and unskilled workers—a structure that may seem unexpected at first glance. The skilled members included electricians, I&C (instrumentation and control) technicians, welders, plumbers, pipefitters, gantry crane operators, and millwrights, while the unskilled members consisted of security personnel, janitors, clerks, general maintenance workers, tour guides, and warehousemen.

Company C was a power generation facility, requiring both skilled and unskilled labor to maintain and operate the site safely. The work environment was hazardous, but cleanliness was a constant priority in nearly all areas. Before I delve into my experiences and challenges, it is important to provide some context on the IBEW.

The International Brotherhood of Electrical Workers (IBEW)

The IBEW is one of the most influential labor unions in North America, representing electrical workers across industries such as construction, utilities, manufacturing, and telecommunications. The union plays a critical role in setting industry standards for safety, training, and workforce development. Established in 1891, the IBEW originally aimed to address hazardous working conditions for early electrical workers as electricity spread across the United States. Today, it boasts over 775,000 active members and retirees across the United States, Canada, and other countries (International Brotherhood of Electrical Workers 2023).

The IBEW's strength lies in its focus on training and safety. In partnership with the National Electrical Contractors Association (NECA), it operates the National Joint Apprenticeship and Training Committee (NJATC), offering world-class training in specializations like electrical installation, telecommunications, and renewable energy systems such as solar and wind power. This extensive training infrastructure, with over 300 centers across North America, ensures that IBEW members remain some of the most skilled and safety-conscious workers in the industry (NJATC 2022).

The IBEW has been an active advocate for workers' rights and safety regulations. It negotiates CBAs that provide competitive wages, retirement benefits, healthcare, and protections against unfair labor practices. Moreover, the IBEW has taken a leadership role in promoting job creation in emerging industries, such as renewable energy. By preparing its members for these future demands, the union has remained central to both the electrical and broader energy industries (AFL-CIO 2022).

My Role at Company C

I began my tenure at Company C as a supervisor overseeing electricians, a role I held for 2 years before advancing to operations supervisor and outage coordinator. The IBEW at Company C wielded significant influence, commanding respect from both union members and management. Navigating this dynamic workforce required a different level of preparedness compared to my previous roles. Fortunately, my predecessor trained me for several months, easing my transition from managing a weaker union, the United Steelworkers (USW), to the more robust IBEW. My predecessor was meticulous, documenting everything and mastering the contract, which he encouraged me to do as well. Following his example, I diligently documented incidents, studied the contract, and maintained consistency in my management approach. Notably, later in my career at Company C, I served on the committee that helped revise the contract.

One of the most valuable experiences in my first 6 months was attending Labor Relations Training (MARC—shown in the image below). This training, which I highly recommend to anyone supervising union employees, prepared me for real-world scenarios through mock grievance meetings, investigative discussions, and role-playing. It also reinforced the importance of thoroughly understanding the contract, an invaluable skill for anyone in management. After this training, I felt confident with 12 years of experience managing union employees. However, I soon learned that no amount of training or experience could have fully prepared me for managing a union working without a contract (Figure 6.1).

Managing Unionized Labor Without a Negotiated Contract

Managing a workforce without a negotiated contract presented challenges unlike anything I had encountered before. When Company C and the union failed to reach a new agreement, the workforce continued operating under the previous contract, a practice referred to as "working without a contract." However, in reality, this meant working under protest, adding tension to daily operations. I was surprised to learn that some

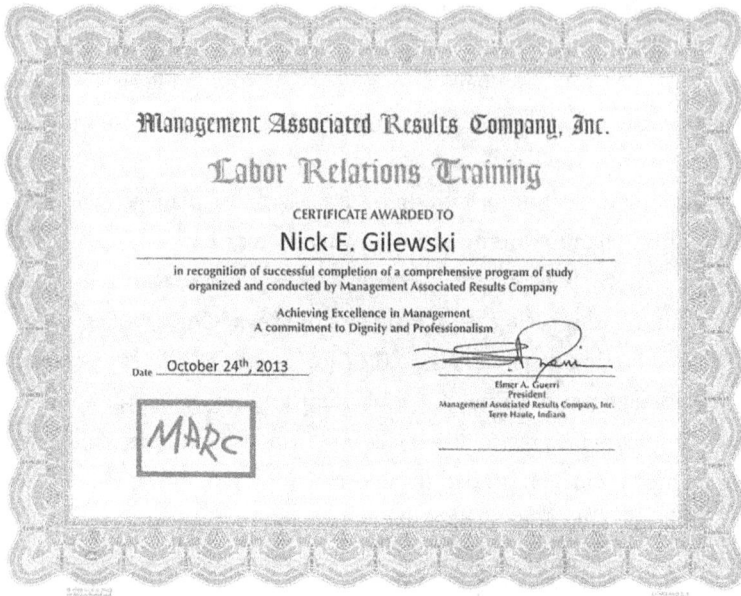

Figure 6.1 Labor relations training certificate

unions, including the IBEW at Company C, are legally prohibited from striking, which, while beneficial for public safety, significantly complicates labor relations.

The union continued to work under the old contract, a practice they referred to as "working without a contract." Although this term was repeated often, the reality was that they were working under protest. Importantly, safety was always prioritized, and professionalism was mostly maintained by both management and union members, despite the challenging circumstances.

During this period, however, certain union members occasionally took unconventional actions to express their dissatisfaction with the impasse. One such incident stands out in my memory: While heading to a jobsite with a mechanical supervisor, we heard a loud thud from the back of our company truck. Upon investigation, we found a 12-pound bowling ball rolling around. This odd occurrence was an example of how the union expressed its frustration, hoping that such acts would send a message to upper management.

Overtime and Tactics During the Impasse

Overtime is often a sensitive issue, but during a contract impasse, it became an even greater source of contention. The absence of a new contract meant stagnant wages and no additional benefits, leaving employees frustrated. As a result, workers strategically used slowdowns and procedural stand-downs to amplify pressure on management, aiming to accelerate negotiations. Skilled workers, in particular, used various tactics to slow down work, hoping to force supervisors like myself to pressure upper management into reaching a contract agreement.

For example, the union steward would regularly halt work, citing safety concerns, even when the job had been done many times before without issue. This would necessitate safety evaluations, causing delays. Other workers would arrive at jobsites only to claim they lacked the necessary parts or refuse to proceed without a work order, further dragging out the process. These tactics led to more overtime, a way for workers to compensate for the lack of pay increases.

As a supervisor, I had to navigate these challenges carefully. I adhered strictly to the rules, knowing that any deviation could lead to grievances. In one instance, I received a grievance for simply using a tape measure, a task designated for engineers. On another occasion, frustration resulted after I guided electricians through troubleshooting that shortened the job's duration, because it reduced their overtime hours.

Differences Between Skilled and Unskilled Labor During an Impasse

The operational impact of a contract impasse varied between skilled and unskilled labor. While both groups could engage in slowdowns, skilled workers had a more direct influence on production. If electricians, millwrights, or I&C technicians delayed critical repairs, operations could grind to a halt. In contrast, delays in tasks performed by janitorial or general maintenance staff, while disruptive, had a less immediate effect on productivity. Unskilled workers, such as janitors or maintenance staff, are essential, but their actions did not directly affect core operations like skilled workers did. For example, if equipment wasn't repaired, production could come to a halt, but if cleaning took longer, the impact was minimal. I mean no disrespect to unskilled workers; I am simply stating my objective experience and observation.

This distinction is important for anyone managing unionized labor. Understanding the varying impacts of different roles helps managers respond appropriately to work slowdowns and other tactics.

The IBEW Apprenticeship Program

Finally, I want to highlight the IBEW's apprenticeship program, which I believe is one of the most effective ways to promote from within. At Company C, most union members started in unskilled positions, such as security or janitorial roles. My predecessor, for instance, had started as a janitor and eventually worked his way up to supervising electricians over a 10-year period.

The IBEW apprenticeship program at Company C was a comprehensive, performance-driven initiative designed to develop skilled professionals. It required apprentices to meet stringent benchmarks in technical knowledge, hands-on experience, and adherence to safety protocols. A joint labor–management committee ensured accountability, with progress meticulously tracked through sign-offs from union trainers and supervisors. It was overseen by a joint union–management committee, and each task completed by an apprentice had to be signed off by the union member, the trainer, and the supervisor. It was incredibly encouraging to see workers progress through the program and advance in their careers.

Conclusion

My time at Company C, working with the IBEW, was one of the most transformative phases of my career. Managing skilled labor during a contract impasse forced me to refine my leadership approach, balancing firm adherence to policy with an acute awareness of workforce dynamics. I gained a deeper understanding of how morale, communication, and strategic negotiation shape labor relations in high-stakes environments. The experience underscored the intricate connection between employee morale and operational efficiency; when workers are dissatisfied, their actions, whether intentional slowdowns or procedural stand-downs, can impact productivity and workplace atmosphere. Understanding this connection helped me appreciate the broader implications of unresolved grievances and motivated me to prioritize open, respectful communication.

One of my most valuable takeaways from Company C was the importance of adapting my management style to fit the unique conditions of the workforce. A rigid, authoritative approach would have been ineffective and could have worsened tensions during the impasse. Instead, I learned that patience, adherence to procedures, and clear communication were essential in navigating a contentious work environment. By following established protocols and maintaining a collaborative stance, I was able to foster a sense of stability, even when emotions ran high.

The experience also deepened my respect for the IBEW's apprenticeship program. Seeing union members grow and advance through a structured, well-supported process reinforced the importance of career development within the organization. Investing in training and promoting from within proved to be an effective way to build a skilled, committed workforce, which is especially critical in high-stakes industries like power generation.

Finally, my time at Company C highlighted the varying operational impact of skilled and unskilled labor. Recognizing the unique contributions of each group helped me respond effectively to challenges while maintaining morale. Every role is vital, yet skilled labor often has a more immediate effect on production—a dynamic that taught me the value of managing each group with tailored strategies.

In conclusion, the lessons from Company C taught me that effective management in unionized environments relies on a balance of firmness, fairness, and empathy, always grounded in an unwavering commitment to safety. For leaders stepping into similar roles, my advice is to prioritize labor relations training, build a strong understanding of the contract, and invest time in relationship-building. Though there will be challenges and setbacks, approaching the role with resilience, respect, and a deep understanding of both the workforce and the contractual framework can lead to meaningful progress. Company C and the IBEW shaped me into a more thoughtful, adaptive leader, and for that, I am deeply grateful.

For supervisors, this chapter highlights the importance of consistency, contract mastery, and relationship-building with union representatives.

For HR professionals, navigating a contract impasse requires balancing structured policies with an awareness of workforce sentiment while ensuring grievances do not escalate into productivity losses. For business leaders, understanding the operational impact of skilled versus unskilled labor during disputes can drive more effective workforce planning and negotiation strategies. Regardless of your role, this chapter demonstrates that managing unionized labor is not just about enforcing rules. It is about fostering collaboration, ensuring safety, and maintaining respect between management and employees.

CHAPTER 7

Managing Unionized Engineers in the Utility Sector

Introduction to Company D and the UWUA

For *supervisors* managing professional unionized employees, *HR professionals* overseeing structured labor agreements, and *business leaders* making strategic workforce decisions, this chapter provides key insights into managing engineers within a strong union framework. My experience at Company D, an electric distribution company in New York City, was unique compared to my previous roles because it was entirely office-based, yet strictly governed by the Utility Workers Union of America (UWUA). Managing unionized engineers required a balance of technical expertise, adherence to structured processes, and a methodical approach to labor relations. Whether you are navigating union contracts, handling digital communication in a remote work environment, or managing highly educated professionals within a union setting, this chapter provides valuable lessons on leadership, contract compliance, and maintaining professional relationships in a nonindustrial setting.

At Company D, I was responsible for managing projects and a team of engineers. These engineers went through a rigorous process to become Senior Engineers, which was achieved through the union. When hired, they started as apprentices, and after 1 year of on-the-job training, they took a test that determined if they would be moved up in pay and title. The entire process took 8 years to become a Senior Engineer. When I heard the term "engineer," I initially thought of an exempt employee. However, this was not the case, as the engineers working for me were union members. Despite this, it was the best relationship I had with union members—it felt almost as if they were not union at all. This may have been because we shared a similar background, as I am an engineer as well.

Company D was not a production or operating facility; rather, it was based in an office setting. The union employees I managed were electrical engineers, which at times seemed counterintuitive, as they might typically be considered exempt by their titles. Most employees dressed in khaki pants and button-down shirts. All of their work was done on computers, and they rarely went into the field. The UWUA was very strict and comparable to Companies A and C. There was a union steward and a union president on our floor for the engineers, and a formal contract was followed meticulously. Before sharing my union challenges and experiences, it is best to provide some background and information about the UWUA.

Background on the UWUA

The UWUA is a prominent labor union that represents workers in the utility sector, including electricity, gas, water, and nuclear energy industries. Established in 1945, the UWUA was formed to unify and provide a collective voice for utility workers, advocating for better wages, benefits, and safety standards. Today, the UWUA has more than 50,000 members across the United States, working in various roles, including power generation, transmission, and distribution, as well as water treatment and gas supply. The union is affiliated with the AFL-CIO (American Federation of Labor and Congress of Industrial Organizations), providing it with a broad network and significant influence in labor-related issues (Utility Workers Union of America 2023).

The UWUA is particularly known for its strong focus on workplace safety, given the high-risk nature of utility work. The union plays an active role in negotiating and enforcing safety protocols for its members, particularly those working in hazardous environments such as power plants and gas utilities. One of the union's key programs is its Power for America Training Trust Fund (P4A), which offers extensive training and apprenticeship programs aimed at improving both safety and technical skills. This initiative helps ensure that utility workers are equipped to handle the rapidly evolving technologies in the energy sector, including the integration of renewable energy sources like wind and solar into traditional utility grids (Power for America Training Trust Fund 2025).

In addition to collective bargaining, the UWUA has been heavily involved in political advocacy. The union actively supports legislation that promotes job security, fair wages, and the expansion of clean energy initiatives. For example, the UWUA has been a strong proponent of the Green New Deal and other climate-focused policies, arguing that they will create new jobs in the energy sector while protecting existing utility jobs. The UWUA's political engagement extends to lobbying for infrastructure investments and job protections in the face of industry deregulation, making it a key player in both the labor and energy sectors (Utility Workers Union of America 2023).

Managing an Office-Based Unionized Team

The leadership style I used at Company D was tailored for an office environment that was unionized, and the union employees were highly professional. The employees were skilled in that they had a formal college education, mostly in engineering. In addition to their college education, they had to complete an apprenticeship program involving varying degrees of engineering experience. To become a top-paid engineer, it took 8 years and required passing a test. This path was comparable to that of a journeyman electrician or plumber, except that the pay grade was higher due to the college degree.

There were other union members outside of the building working in the field, including typical journeyman electricians. I did not have the opportunity to manage these journeyman electricians directly, but I made connections with those who did, and they were part of a strong union that followed the contract exclusively. During my time at Company D, I received two grievances regarding overtime, with employees claiming that they were skipped over and that others were receiving preferential treatment. Both grievances were resolved at the B step by printing out the overtime records and sharing them with the union steward and the employee. Everything was handled formally, with no direct dealing, and it was done through a steward.

One particularly challenging situation involved writing up an employee for inappropriate emails, which violated the company's code of conduct. Since most of the communication at Company D was done via email and messages, proper communication was vital to management. Keep in mind this was after 2020, when almost everything went online, and nearly all communication became digital. Therefore, it was crucial to be careful with what you said and how you said it. Meetings were conducted online, and participants did not have to be on camera. The engineers could work from home 2 days a week and were required to be in the office three days a week. The initial decision to work from home was negotiated by the union, and, therefore, any changes to this arrangement had to be negotiated.

The written warning for the inappropriate emails was handled formally, with a union steward and the employee present. Additionally, I had another manager with me in the room as a scribe and witness. The steward and employee became heated and wanted to discuss the details further, but I presented the facts and was disinclined to entertain further discussions. This method of dealing was learned from many write-ups and sit-downs with union stewards, presidents, and employees. I have learned to revert to the facts, avoid subjectivity, and stay on point. I do not get caught up in minutiae because it is in the best interest of both myself and the employee. Early in my career, I would get caught in debates that became heated, making situations and relationships worse. I now avoid that at all costs—zero tolerance.

This environment required a more methodical approach compared to my previous positions. Given the nature of the work, I had to rely heavily on documentation, ensuring every action taken was recorded meticulously. The engineers were diligent, and they expected management to hold themselves to similar standards. This transparency in recordkeeping and communication helped build trust and also served as an essential tool during grievance processes. The office environment, while less physically demanding than a production setting, brought its own unique stressors related to precision and accountability.

Conclusion

Managing a unionized team of engineers in an office-based utility environment presented unique challenges and learning opportunities. Unlike my previous roles, this setting required a high degree of formality and precision in all interactions. The engineers were highly skilled professionals who expected clear, objective, and fair management practices while leveraging the contract when needed. This experience underscored the importance of professionalism and transparency in maintaining positive union–management relations.

One key takeaway from Company D was the necessity of adhering closely to formal processes, particularly in scheduling, overtime allocation, and disciplinary actions. Unlike production environments where extended shifts were common, the engineers followed strict schedules, requiring full transparency and contract adherence for any adjustments. This emphasis on time management reinforced the need to anticipate and plan for overtime well in advance.

The shift to digital communication added another layer of complexity. With remote work and online meetings becoming the norm post-2020, careful attention to tone and clarity became essential. Email and messaging replaced many in-person discussions, necessitating a fact-based, professional approach to prevent misinterpretations. Digital records also introduced new accountability standards, reinforcing the value of precise, objective communication that could be referenced later.

Additionally, having a witness or second manager present during formal disciplinary actions added accountability and transparency for both the management and the union. The union steward's presence ensured adherence to established procedures, while a second manager provided impartial oversight. This structured approach fostered trust and professionalism in otherwise challenging situations.

One of the most positive aspects of my role at Company D was the collaborative relationship I built with the engineers. Our shared technical background created a foundation of mutual respect and effective communication, particularly when addressing complex engineering challenges. Unlike past experiences where union relations were often contentious, this role fostered a sense of partnership, leading to smoother negotiations and daily interactions.

Ultimately, my time at Company D marked the culmination of lessons learned throughout my career. From strict adherence to processes to the value of relationship-building within a unionized environment, this experience refined my approach to managing skilled labor. The combination of technical expertise, professionalism, and respect for union representation created a fulfilling and successful chapter in my journey of managing unionized teams.

CHAPTER 8

Summary of Experiences and Core Principles for Supervising Unionized Workers

Introduction

After managing unionized workforces across four distinct roles and industries, one truth stands clear: leadership within union environments is as much about understanding people and relationships as it is about interpreting contracts. Each of my roles shaped a different part of my leadership philosophy, exposing unique challenges that, when combined, offered a comprehensive view into what it takes to supervise unionized labor effectively. This chapter distills those lessons not as a repetition of previous chapters but as a practical guide for those who seek to lead with confidence and integrity in unionized settings. To complement these lessons, Table 8.1 at the end of the chapter provides a practical summary of leadership styles tailored to each union I have worked with.

Lesson One: Know the Contract, Respect the Culture (Company A – IAM, IUOE, BCTGM)

My introduction to union leadership taught me that the contract is only half the equation. Yes, it provides structure, but it does not reveal the informal practices, emotional undercurrents, or historical sensitivities that exist within a unionized team. Early missteps, like jumping in to help troubleshoot equipment, were met with formal grievances because I misunderstood the significance of clearly defined roles. I learned that respecting union culture was not just a courtesy; it was a requirement for earning trust.

Lesson Two: Lead Beside Them, but Maintain the Line (Company B – USW)

Transitioning to Company B, I entered a foundry environment—a dangerous, high-risk setting, working with the United Steelworkers (USW). The foundry demanded physical toughness, and the camaraderie among workers was palpable. Compared to my previous role, the union presence at this facility was weaker, which afforded me a different kind of flexibility in managing union relationships. For example, I was able to establish training programs and even create work schedules without the formal involvement of union leadership—something that would have been impossible at Company A.

The foundry taught me that leadership was not just about giving orders. At times, I found myself side by side with workers, wielding tools in the furnace or operating machinery, actions that would typically be outside the scope of a manager in a strictly unionized setting. This experience helped me forge deep connections with the workforce. However, I also learned that there were dangers in blurring lines between labor and management, as it could lead to confusion over boundaries and authority.

Lesson Three: Remain Calm During Contractual Chaos (Company C – IBEW)

Managing during a contract impasse was one of the most difficult challenges of my career. Skilled union members used every legitimate means to express discontent, including prolonged safety stand-downs, strategic work slowdowns, and frequent procedural inquiries. In this environment, emotional restraint and operational discipline were essential. I could not afford to make reactionary decisions. I had to become meticulous with documentation and unwavering in my consistency. From this experience, I learned that leadership under pressure is not about control; it is about composure.

Lesson Four: Communicate with Precision and Professionalism (Company D – UWUA)

Supervising unionized engineers was unlike any other role. The environment was formal, structured, and highly professional. Every word mattered, whether spoken or written. These engineers knew the contract in detail and were not hesitant to cite it. I learned to craft every email, directive, and conversation with clarity and forethought. This role refined my communication skills and taught me that leadership in a professional union setting requires not only knowledge but also a disciplined and strategic voice.

Guiding Principles for Supervising Unionized Workers

Across my four supervisory roles managing unionized labor, several key lessons emerged that shaped my leadership approach:

1. **Respect for Union Roles and Boundaries**: Understanding and respecting the distinct roles within union environments is critical. Overstepping boundaries, even with good intentions, can lead to grievances and erode trust.
2. **Adaptability of Leadership Styles**: Different work environments— from automated production lines to dangerous foundries, from power generation to office settings—required me to adapt my leadership style. A directive approach might work in nonunion settings, but a collaborative, empathetic style was essential for managing unionized teams.
3. **The Importance of Fairness and Consistency**: Unionized workers value consistency above all else. Whether it was managing overtime or handling grievances, maintaining a fair and consistent approach helped me build credibility and trust.
4. **The Power of Empathy and Relationship-Building**: Building strong relationships with union members was central to my success. Being visible, approachable, and willing to admit mistakes allowed me to earn the respect of my teams over time.

5. **Navigating Grievances and Contractual Challenges**: Managing grievances was an inevitable part of supervising unionized labor. I learned that the grievance process, while challenging, could also be an opportunity to build respect through transparent communication and adherence to the contract.

Conclusion

This journey has shown me that supervising unionized labor is not about authority. It is about earning influence through consistency, empathy, and preparation. Each unionized environment required a different leadership posture, but the outcome was always the same: when respect is mutual and processes are followed with integrity, union and management can move forward together.

Whether you are entering your first union supervisory role or refining your approach after years of experience, these lessons provide a foundation you can build upon. The work is demanding, but the rewards—respect, trust, and team cohesion—are well worth the effort.

To further support readers, Table 8.1 provides a comparative summary of leadership styles that proved most effective across the various unions I have worked with, including IAM, BCTGM, IUOE, USW, IBEW, and UWUA. This table is designed as a practical reference to help managers understand which leadership approach best aligns with each union's unique culture, structure, and operational context.

Table 8.1 Leadership styles for IAM, BCT, IOUE, IBEW, USW, and UWUA

Union	Leadership style	Application to skilled workers
IAM (International Association of Machinists and Aerospace Workers)	Transformational	Inspire skilled workers by setting a clear vision, promoting continuous improvement, and encouraging adaptability. *Skilled machinists value respect and motivation to achieve collective goals.* This style involves fostering a culture of innovation and empowerment, enabling machinists to feel personally invested in the success of their work and the organization. Regular feedback sessions and recognition of achievements can further reinforce their commitment.

Union	Leadership style	Application to skilled workers
BCTGM (Bakery, Confectionery, Tobacco Workers, and Grain Millers)	Participative	Involve skilled workers in decision-making processes. This collaborative approach can increase engagement among workers, who often have specific knowledge about production quality and safety. Participative leadership empowers workers to share their insights, leading to better problem-solving and a sense of ownership in their tasks. By encouraging open dialogue and valuing their contributions, leaders can build trust and improve morale. *Regular team meetings and suggestion programs can be effective tools for implementing this approach.*
IOUE (International Union of Operating Engineers)	Directive	Provide clear instructions and safety-focused guidance, crucial for operating complex machinery. Skilled operators benefit from structured leadership, especially in hazardous work environments. A directive approach ensures that tasks are performed consistently and safely, minimizing risks associated with heavy equipment. *This style is particularly effective when quick, decisive action is required.* Detailed standard operating procedures (SOPs), regular safety briefings, and close supervision can help maintain high safety and performance standards.
IBEW (International Brotherhood of Electrical Workers)	Coaching	Focus on skill development and mentorship. *Skilled electricians respond well to coaching that enhances their technical expertise and supports ongoing certification or training requirements.* Coaching leadership involves identifying individual strengths and areas for improvement, providing tailored guidance, and fostering a culture of continuous learning. This approach can help electricians stay up-to-date with evolving technologies and industry standards. Hands-on training sessions, mentorship programs, and constructive feedback are key components of effective coaching in this context.

(continued)

Table 8.1 Leadership styles for IAM, BCT, IOUE, IBEW, USW, and UWUA (continued)

Union	Leadership style	Application to skilled workers
USW (United Steelworkers)	Transactional	Emphasize clear expectations and rewards for meeting performance standards. Skilled steelworkers benefit from knowing the precise requirements of their roles and the incentives associated with meeting those requirements. *Transactional leadership works well in environments where tasks are routine and require adherence to strict guidelines.* Regular performance evaluations and a system of rewards for meeting safety and production targets can help maintain motivation and compliance.
UWUA (Utility Workers Union of America)	**Servant Leadership**	Prioritize the needs of utility workers by ensuring their safety, well-being, and access to resources. *Skilled utility workers appreciate a leader who supports them in providing essential services.* Servant leadership emphasizes empathy, listening, and addressing workers' concerns, which can lead to higher job satisfaction and loyalty. Leaders who practice servant leadership often focus on removing obstacles that hinder workers' ability to perform their duties effectively. Providing proper equipment, advocating for worker rights, and fostering a supportive work environment are crucial elements of this leadership style. Regular check-ins and opportunities for workers to voice their needs can further strengthen this approach.

PART 3

Industry Insights and Future Trends

CHAPTER 9

Effective Management Strategies for Unionized Labor

Managing unionized labor requires a strategic balance of collaboration, consistency, and respect for CBAs. Whether you are a *frontline supervisor*, *an HR professional* responsible for labor relations, or a business leader overseeing unionized operations, this chapter provides essential management strategies to foster trust, enhance workplace safety, and maintain compliance. A strong foundation of trust between management and unionized employees not only improves morale but also contributes to a safer, more efficient work environment. By applying these approaches, managers can navigate the complexities of unionized workplaces while ensuring operational efficiency and workforce well-being.

Building Collaborative Relationships

Establishing open and trustworthy relationships with union representatives and employees is fundamental to effective management. Proactive engagement helps prevent conflicts and cultivates a positive workplace culture, demonstrating a commitment to shared goals.

1. **Engage Regularly with Union Representatives**
   Regular meetings with union representatives provide a platform to address workplace concerns, identify potential issues early, and foster mutual understanding. These discussions offer opportunities to communicate upcoming projects, policy changes, and other important updates, creating a space for transparency and collaboration.

2. **Participate in Joint Committees**
   Joint labor–management committees offer a collaborative venue for tackling shared priorities like safety, productivity, and training. Active involvement in these committees not only builds trust but also reinforces management's dedication to common goals, aligning efforts with union interests.

3. **Respect Union Contracts and Boundaries**
   Adhering strictly to the CBA is essential to maintaining credibility. Following the CBA's guidelines demonstrates respect for negotiated terms and establishes consistency, reducing the likelihood of disputes and fostering respect between management and employees.

Implementing Fair and Transparent Policies

Transparent and consistently applied policies promote trust and minimize misunderstandings. Ensuring clear communication and enforcement of policies helps create a level-playing field and reinforces organizational stability.

1. **Develop Detailed Job Descriptions**
   Clear job descriptions help clarify roles and responsibilities, preventing conflicts and ensuring employees understand their expectations. This can preempt issues related to job duties, which is essential for cohesive operations.

2. **Apply Policies Consistently**
   Consistency in policy enforcement across the organization eliminates perceptions of favoritism. This consistency is particularly important in areas like attendance, performance evaluations, and disciplinary actions, which affect morale and team dynamics.

3. **Maintain Open Channels for Communication**
   Regular team meetings, open-door policies, and accessible suggestion boxes encourage employees to share concerns and insights. These channels allow management to stay attuned to employee needs, fostering a workplace culture that values transparency and active communication.

Addressing Grievances Efficiently

Handling grievances effectively is essential to maintaining union processes and reinforcing management's commitment to fairness. A streamlined grievance process prevents escalations, preserves morale, and strengthens trust.

1. **Establish a Clear Grievance Procedure**
   A structured grievance process, with clearly outlined steps, provides employees with a reliable method for raising concerns. Clearly communicating this procedure promotes understanding and contributes to the swift resolution of issues.

2. **Provide Grievance Management Training for Supervisors**
   Equipping supervisors with grievance management training—including confidentiality, respectful engagement, and issue resolution techniques—ensures consistency and reinforces a fair approach to handling complaints.

3. **Prioritize Swift, Fair Resolutions**
   Prompt resolution of grievances demonstrates respect for employee concerns and minimizes disruptions. Resolving grievances promptly and fairly strengthens trust and prevents lingering frustrations, promoting a balanced work environment.

Promoting Continuous Learning and Development

Ongoing investment in employee development enhances workforce competitiveness and strengthens employee loyalty. This approach is key to retaining skilled employees and adapting to changes in the industry.

1. **Provide Targeted Training Programs**
   Specialized training in technical skills, safety practices, and leadership helps keep employees' competencies up-to-date. Regular training aligns employee growth with organizational needs, enhancing both productivity and job satisfaction.

2. **Support Apprenticeship and Mentorship Initiatives**
   Apprenticeship programs offer hands-on experience that builds confidence and nurtures skilled labor pipelines. Mentorship

opportunities provide career guidance, which enhances job satisfaction and encourages skill transfer among team members.

3. **Encourage Ongoing Professional Development**
   Offering opportunities for certifications, conferences, and specialized courses shows employees that their growth is valued. This commitment encourages employees to stay, grow, and contribute meaningfully to the organization.

Ensuring Workplace Safety

Prioritizing workplace safety is crucial in managing unionized skilled labor. Strong safety protocols, proactive compliance, and a focus on hazard prevention protect workers and foster a culture of safety consciousness.

1. **Conduct Regular Safety Training**
   Tailor safety training to address industry-specific risks, ensuring compliance with regulations and reinforcing a culture of safety. This approach also shows management's dedication to employees' well-being.

2. **Implement Routine Safety Audits**
   Regular audits identify potential hazards and verify adherence to safety standards. Including union representatives in these audits promotes a collaborative approach to safety, emphasizing that it is a shared responsibility.

3. **Encourage Hazard Reporting Without Retaliation**
   A culture that supports hazard reporting without fear of retaliation is crucial to maintaining a safe work environment. This proactive approach helps mitigate risks and demonstrates management's commitment to safety.

Fostering Open Communication

Open communication is essential to building trust and addressing issues before they escalate. Clear, regular communication between management and employees fosters a positive workplace culture and improves problem-solving.

1. **Hold Regular Team Meetings**
   Regular meetings keep employees informed, encourage engagement, and invite valuable feedback. These sessions allow managers to update employees on operational goals and provide a forum for employee questions and ideas.

2. **Provide Constructive Feedback**
   Regular, constructive feedback enables employees to understand their strengths and areas for improvement, supporting their development. This feedback reinforces expectations and encourages continuous growth.

3. **Seek Employee Input on Policy and Decision Making**
   Involving employees in decisions that affect their work environment fosters a sense of ownership. This approach respects their insights, increases commitment to organizational goals, and enhances overall engagement.

Leveraging Union Expertise

Union representatives offer valuable expertise, particularly in safety, training, and worker advocacy. Collaborating with unions to leverage their resources can improve working conditions, boost employee satisfaction, and strengthen labor–management relations.

1. **Collaborate on Specialized Training Programs**
   Many unions provide training that enhances members' skills and safety. Collaborating with unions to offer these programs to employees benefits both the workforce and the organization.

2. **Include Union Input in Policy Development**
   Seeking union representatives' perspectives on policy decisions ensures alignment with workforce needs. This collaborative approach fosters smoother policy implementation and aligns with employee expectations.

3. **Partner on Safety and Wellness Initiatives**
   Collaborative safety programs with union involvement strengthen workplace safety initiatives. These partnerships foster shared

responsibility, improve compliance, and promote a culture of well-being throughout the workforce.

Conclusion

Successfully managing unionized labor requires a balance of collaboration, transparency, and a steadfast commitment to safety and employee development. Building strong relationships with union representatives, implementing fair and consistent policies, efficiently addressing grievances, supporting continuous learning, and maintaining open communication channels are all vital components of successful management. Additionally, leveraging union expertise, particularly in training and safety, demonstrates respect for the union's role and contributes to a harmonious work environment.

The strategies outlined in this chapter serve as a practical framework for navigating the complexities of unionized labor management, fostering trust, improving employee satisfaction, and advancing organizational goals. By respecting union structures, adhering to established protocols, and prioritizing employee well-being, managers can lead cooperative workplaces where unionized labor thrives.

The next chapter presents case studies and real-world examples that illustrate these strategies in action. These examples illustrate the nuances and challenges of managing unionized labor, demonstrating how the strategies discussed here can be successfully applied in diverse, dynamic settings. Through these case studies, insights into the practical realities of union–management relations are revealed and a firsthand look at how effective strategies can lead to lasting positive outcomes is provided.

CHAPTER 10

Case Studies and Real-World Examples

Successfully managing unionized labor requires a strategic balance of collaboration, communication, and adherence to structured labor agreements. This chapter provides real-world case studies that highlight the complexities of managing unionized labor across different industries. Whether you are a *supervisor*, *HR professional*, or *business leader*, these examples illustrate best practices, challenges, and lessons that can help in fostering strong union–management relationships and improving operational efficiency.

Each case study showcases different union dynamics and management strategies, illustrating both effective collaboration models and the consequences of poor labor relations. The goal is to equip leaders with actionable insights that can be applied across manufacturing, construction, healthcare, and utilities.

Case Study 1: Manufacturing Industry, Ford Motor Company—A Collaborative Approach to Managing Unionized Skilled Labor

Ford Motor Company, one of the largest and oldest automotive manufacturers in the world, has a longstanding relationship with the United Auto Workers (UAW), one of the most powerful labor unions in the United States. Since the 1940s. Ford has worked closely with the UAW to create a collaborative environment that supports both the company's goals and the rights of its workers. Over the years, Ford has used a combination of open communication, joint labor–management committees, and employee training programs to successfully manage its unionized skilled workforce (Ford Motor Company and UAW Collaboration 2008).

Key Strategies:

1. Joint Labor–Management Committees: Ford established joint labor–management committees with the UAW to address workplace issues such as safety, training, and productivity. These committees were particularly instrumental during times of economic uncertainty, such as the financial crisis of 2008 when Ford and the UAW worked together to ensure job security while maintaining operational efficiency. The committees allowed both sides to have open communication about challenges and solutions, fostering a cooperative relationship.

2. Continuous Improvement Programs: Ford integrated lean manufacturing principles and other continuous improvement programs into their production processes. Rather than excluding the UAW from these initiatives, Ford involved the union in discussions about how to optimize efficiency without sacrificing worker well-being. This collaboration helped secure UAW support for changes that improved production quality while maintaining fair labor practices.

3. Employee Training and Development: Ford has invested heavily in training and development programs for its unionized workforce. The company worked with the UAW to create apprenticeship programs and technical training courses that allowed workers to advance their skills in areas such as robotics, automation, and vehicle electrification. These programs have helped Ford adapt to technological advancements while ensuring that unionized employees remain competitive and valuable to the company's future growth.

4. Collaborative Bargaining: Ford and the UAW have maintained a strong collaborative bargaining approach, especially in negotiations concerning wages, benefits, and working conditions. During contract negotiations, both sides focus on long-term sustainability, ensuring that agreements support Ford's business strategy while protecting the interests of its skilled labor force.

Outcomes and Lessons Learned:

- Improved Productivity and Efficiency: By involving the UAW in continuous improvement programs, Ford was able to enhance productivity and streamline operations without facing significant resistance from its skilled workforce. The collaborative efforts helped reduce production costs while improving product quality.

- Workplace Safety Improvements: Ford and the UAW's joint focus on safety resulted in numerous improvements in safety protocols and a reduction in workplace accidents. Ford's safety programs, including ergonomics training and regular safety audits, were implemented with the full cooperation of union representatives.
- Enhanced Employee Engagement: The collaborative relationship between Ford and the UAW fostered a positive work environment where unionized workers felt valued and heard. This engagement contributed to lower turnover rates and higher job satisfaction.
- Navigating Economic Downturns: During the 2008 financial crisis, Ford and the UAW worked together to avoid bankruptcy by agreeing to wage concessions and restructuring plans. This cooperation allowed Ford to weather the crisis without the major layoffs and closures that other automakers faced, preserving many unionized jobs.

Ford's ability to maintain a strong, collaborative relationship with the UAW demonstrates how effective union management can lead to long-term success in the manufacturing industry. By working together, both Ford and the UAW have been able to navigate economic challenges, technological changes, and global competition, ensuring that the company remains competitive while protecting the interests of its skilled labor force.

Case Study 2: The Big Dig Project—Poor Labor Relations Leading to Delays and Cost Overruns

The Big Dig, officially known as the Central Artery/Tunnel Project, was one of the most ambitious and expensive construction projects in U.S. history. Its goal was to reroute the main highway through the heart of Boston, primarily through tunnels. Managed by the Massachusetts Turnpike Authority, the project involved numerous labor unions and contractors. The project began in 1991 and was supposed to be completed by 1998, but it was not fully finished until 2007, and its costs ballooned from an initial estimate of $2.8 billion to over $15 billion. The project's extensive delays and cost overruns were exacerbated by poor labor relations, mismanagement, and frequent conflicts between contractors, labor unions, and government entities (Massachusetts Turnpike Authority 2007).

Key Issues in Labor Relations:

1. **Lack of Communication and Collaboration**: The Big Dig's construction involved multiple labor unions, including the International Brotherhood of Electrical Workers (IBEW), Laborers' International Union of North America (LIUNA), and the International Union of Operating Engineers (IUOE). There was a significant lack of communication between these unions and project managers. The coordination between contractors and unions was poor, leading to frequent delays and disputes over work assignments.

2. **Jurisdictional Conflict**: One of the major issues in the Big Dig was the constant disputes over jurisdiction between different unions, particularly regarding specific tasks such as operating heavy machinery, electrical work, and tunneling operations. These disputes often resulted in strikes, work stoppages, and prolonged negotiations, significantly delaying the project.

3. **Inconsistent Policy Enforcement**: Management failed to enforce consistent policies across the various contractors working on the Big Dig. This inconsistency led to perceptions of favoritism, particularly when some unions received higher wages or better working conditions than others. The lack of standardized policies created frustration and low morale among workers, contributing to further delays.

4. **Safety Violations and Inadequate Safety Measures**: The Big Dig also suffered from numerous safety violations, with more than 1,000 injuries recorded during the project. In 2006, a section of the tunnel ceiling collapsed, killing a motorist. Investigations revealed that shortcuts were taken during construction, and safety protocols were not properly enforced. Unions often raised safety concerns,

but management's failure to address them effectively contributed to a tense and confrontational work environment.

Outcomes and Lessons Learned:

- **Significant Project Delays**: Due to frequent labor disputes, jurisdictional conflicts, and strikes, the Big Dig experienced numerous delays, extending the project completion date by nearly a decade. The mismanagement of union relations was a major factor in these delays, as work often ground to a halt during negotiations and protests.
- **Massive Cost Overruns**: The original budget for the Big Dig was $2.8 billion, but by the time the project was completed, the total cost had exceeded $15 billion. The prolonged labor disputes, combined with mismanagement and safety failures, contributed significantly to these cost overruns.
- **Low Worker Morale**: Workers often felt undervalued due to the lack of communication and inconsistent treatment among the different unions. This created a negative atmosphere, leading to inefficiency and a lack of cohesion among the labor force. Strikes and protests became common during the course of the project.
- **Legal and Regulatory Issues**: Following the ceiling collapse and safety violations, multiple lawsuits were filed against the contractors, and extensive investigations were conducted by regulatory agencies. The project became infamous for its safety failures, ultimately tarnishing the reputations of the management team and contractors involved.

The Big Dig serves as a cautionary tale in the construction industry. The failure to manage labor relations effectively, combined with poor communication, safety lapses, and inconsistent policies, led to severe delays and cost overruns. The project highlights the critical importance of strong labor–management collaboration, especially when dealing with large-scale projects involving multiple unions and contractors.

Case Study 3: Kaiser Permanente—Collaborative Union–Management Relationship in Healthcare

Kaiser Permanente, one of the largest healthcare organizations in the United States, has been a model for successful collaboration between management and labor unions. With over 160,000 unionized employees, including nurses, technicians, and administrative staff, Kaiser has established a strong partnership with the Coalition of Kaiser Permanente Unions (CKPU). This partnership began with the creation of the Labor Management Partnership (LMP) in 1997, a pioneering initiative designed to promote collaboration, resolve disputes, and improve patient care while addressing employee concerns (Kaiser Permanente 2019).

Key Management Strategies:

1. **Collaborative Decision Making**: The LMP empowered union representatives and management to work together on important decisions related to staffing, patient care, and workplace policies. This collaborative approach helped address concerns before they escalated and ensured that employee voices were heard in shaping operational policies.

   ○ Kaiser's LMP teams consist of frontline workers, union representatives, and management who meet regularly to discuss issues such as staffing shortages, patient safety, and workflow improvements. The collaborative effort aims to align the goals of the union with the operational needs of the healthcare provider.

2. **Professional Development Programs**: Kaiser Permanente invested in comprehensive professional development programs for its unionized staff. These programs focused on career advancement, skill development, and certification in specialized areas of healthcare. Unions and management collaborated to identify critical areas where training was needed to ensure staff stayed up-to-date with medical advancements.

   ○ One standout program was Kaiser's initiative to support union members in earning advanced nursing certifications. This included paid time off for continuing education and mentorship opportunities, which contributed to enhanced patient care quality.

3. **A Focus on Employee Well-Being**: Kaiser Permanente placed a significant emphasis on employee well-being through wellness programs, flexible work schedules, and comprehensive benefits. Union–management cooperation led to the implementation of initiatives aimed at reducing burnout and improving work–life balance, which had a direct positive impact on employee satisfaction and patient outcomes.

   ○ Wellness programs included mental health support services, stress reduction workshops, and access to wellness facilities. Flexible schedules were introduced for nurses and other staff to mitigate high burnout rates commonly seen in the healthcare industry.

Outcomes and Lessons Learned:

- **Improved Patient Care and Outcomes**: The collaboration between Kaiser and the CKPU led to significant improvements in patient care. By engaging frontline workers in decision making, Kaiser was able to streamline processes and improve workflow efficiency, resulting in higher patient satisfaction and better health outcomes. A notable example is the reduction in patient wait times for critical procedures, which was achieved through better staff allocation and management.

- **Enhanced Employee Skills and Career Progression**: Kaiser Permanente's investment in professional development resulted in a highly skilled workforce. Employees were able to advance their careers through certifications and training programs, leading to a more competent and motivated staff. This, in turn, helped Kaiser maintain high standards of care in an industry constantly evolving with new technologies and practices.

- **Reduced Employee Turnover and Burnout**: The focus on employee well-being and flexible scheduling resulted in lower turnover rates compared to industry standards. Kaiser Permanente successfully reduced burnout among healthcare workers

by addressing their concerns proactively through union–
management collaboration.

- **Increased Employee Satisfaction and Engagement**: The LMP
created an environment of mutual respect and collaboration,
which boosted employee morale. Unionized staff reported higher
levels of job satisfaction, feeling that their voices were not only
heard but also acted upon in critical decision-making processes.

The Kaiser Permanente case demonstrates the positive impact that collaborative union–management relationships can have in the healthcare
industry. By focusing on joint decision making, employee development,
and well-being, Kaiser Permanente has successfully navigated challenges
unique to healthcare, while setting an example for other organizations on
how to foster a harmonious and productive workforce.

Case Study 4: Pacific Gas and Electric Company (PG&E)—Best Practices in Managing Unionized Skilled Labor

Pacific Gas and Electric Company (PG&E) is a major utility provider in
California, serving millions of customers with gas and electric services.
PG&E has a longstanding relationship with the International Brotherhood of Electrical Workers (IBEW Local 1245), representing a large por-
tion of its workforce, including linemen, electricians, and power plant
operators. Over the years, PG&E has implemented best practices in
labor–management collaboration, particularly around workplace safety
and continuous employee training, to improve operational performance
and employee satisfaction (Pacific Gas and Electric Company 2022).

Key Management Strategies:

1. **Comprehensive Training Programs**: PG&E is known for offering
robust training programs for its unionized employees, in collaboration with IBEW. These programs focus on developing technical
expertise in electrical systems, safety protocols, and emerging
technologies such as renewable energy integration. The company

operates training facilities that provide hands-on experience, preparing workers to handle complex electrical grid challenges.

- ○ One of the most prominent programs is the apprenticeship program for electrical line workers, which offers unionized employees the opportunity to receive both classroom and field training. This ensures that PG&E's workforce remains highly skilled and capable of handling the evolving needs of the energy sector.

2. **Collaborative Safety Initiatives**: Safety is a top priority for PG&E, particularly due to the hazardous nature of the utility industry. The company works closely with IBEW to establish rigorous safety standards and conduct regular audits. Both management and union representatives participate in joint safety committees to assess risks and develop preventive measures.

- ○ An example of this collaboration is the "Stop Work" policy, where any worker, regardless of his or her position, can halt operations if he or she identified a safety concern. This policy empowers unionized employees to take an active role in maintaining workplace safety and prevents potential accidents.

3. **Open Communication Channels**: PG&E has established open communication channels with IBEW through regular meetings and union–management forums. These meetings focus on addressing workforce concerns, updating workers on company initiatives, and resolving disputes before they escalate. This open line of communication has been instrumental in fostering trust between union members and management.

- ○ PG&E's Labor–Management Partnership meetings take place quarterly, allowing both sides to review performance metrics, safety concerns, and upcoming operational changes. This transparency helps maintain a cooperative and efficient work environment.

4. **Support for Renewable Energy Transition**: As California moves toward more sustainable energy practices, PG&E and IBEW have worked together to train workers in renewable energy technologies. This collaboration ensures that unionized employees are equipped with the necessary skills to operate and maintain solar,

wind, and battery storage systems, supporting California's renewable energy goals.

Outcomes and Lessons Learned:

- **Improved Safety Performance**: The joint safety initiatives between PG&E and IBEW have led to a significant reduction in workplace accidents. The implementation of safety audits, rigorous training, and the "Stop Work" policy has made safety a shared responsibility across all levels of the organization. This proactive approach has helped PG&E maintain one of the best safety records in the utility industry.
- **Enhanced Employee Skills and Knowledge**: Through continuous training and apprenticeship programs, PG&E has built a highly skilled workforce capable of managing the complexities of modern energy infrastructure. This has not only improved operational efficiency but also ensured that PG&E can remain competitive in an industry that is rapidly transitioning to renewable energy sources.
- **Increased Employee Engagement**: The open communication channels and regular union–management meetings have fostered a collaborative atmosphere, leading to increased engagement among unionized employees. Workers feel empowered to contribute to both operational and safety improvements, resulting in higher job satisfaction and lower turnover rates.
- **Operational Excellence and Reliability**: PG&E's focus on employee development, safety, and collaboration with the IBEW has enabled the company to achieve operational excellence. Despite the challenges posed by California's energy demands and regulatory pressures, PG&E has maintained reliable service for millions of customers while investing in the future of energy delivery.

PG&E's successful management of unionized skilled labor through its partnership with IBEW showcases the importance of collaboration, continuous training, and shared responsibility for safety. The company's approach demonstrates how union–management partnerships can drive operational success and employee well-being in high-stakes industries like utilities.

Conclusion to Case Studies: Insights into Unionized Labor Management Across Industries

The detailed case studies of Ford Motor Company, the Big Dig Project, Kaiser Permanente, and PG&E offer critical insights into the challenges and opportunities associated with managing unionized skilled labor across various industries. Each of these organizations provides valuable lessons about the importance of collaboration, communication, safety, and continuous improvement in maintaining a productive and harmonious relationship between management and labor.

Key Themes and Lessons Learned:

1. **Collaborative Labor–Management Relationships Drive Success:**
   In industries as diverse as healthcare, utilities, and manufacturing, a recurring theme in the successful management of unionized labor is the establishment of collaborative relationships between unions and management. Organizations like Ford Motor Company and Kaiser Permanente demonstrate that involving union representatives in decision-making processes—whether it be through joint committees or formal partnerships—results in more effective problem-solving, better workforce morale, and operational efficiency. These partnerships foster a shared sense of ownership and responsibility, leading to positive outcomes for both the company and its employees.
   In contrast, the Big Dig Project in Boston illustrates the consequences of poor collaboration. The lack of effective communication between contractors, unions, and management led to costly delays, safety violations, and project inefficiencies. This case underscores the importance of open, ongoing dialogue between all stakeholders to avoid costly disruptions in labor-intensive projects.

2. **Investment in Employee Training and Development Is Essential:** Across these case studies, the investment in training and development emerges as a critical factor in maintaining a

skilled and adaptive workforce. Ford's continuous improvement programs and PG&E's apprenticeship programs ensure that their unionized workforce remains competitive in the face of technological change. Particularly in industries that are experiencing rapid advancements—such as the shift to renewable energy in the utility sector or the increasing automation in manufacturing—training is a vital tool for maintaining operational excellence and safeguarding job security for workers.

Organizations that fail to invest in their employee's risk inefficiency and resistance to change. The Big Dig Project suffered from labor disputes partly because of insufficient preparation for new technologies and methods. In contrast, Kaiser Permanente and PG&E have used training not only as a tool for maintaining technical proficiency but also as a way to engage workers in organizational goals, improving both job satisfaction and productivity.

3. **Safety and Well-Being Must Be Prioritized:** Safety plays a fundamental role in managing unionized skilled labor, particularly in industries with high-risk environments like utilities and construction. PG&E's collaboration with IBEW to implement rigorous safety protocols and empower workers with the "Stop Work" policy has led to a significant reduction in accidents. Similarly, Kaiser Permanente's wellness programs for employees reduced burnout and ensured a healthier, more motivated workforce.

   On the other hand, the Big Dig Project serves as a reminder of the dangers of neglecting safety. With over 1,000 injuries during construction and a tragic tunnel collapse, the project demonstrated the costly consequences—both human and financial—of failing to establish robust safety measures in collaboration with unions. These examples reinforce the necessity of making safety an integral part of labor–management partnerships, where both parties are actively engaged in identifying risks and implementing preventive measures.

4. **Flexibility and Adaptation Are Key in Navigating Industry Challenges:** The changing economic and technological landscape, particularly the shift toward renewable energy and digitalization, is a major challenge for many industries. PG&E's proactive approach to transitioning its workforce toward renewable energy

technologies, with full collaboration from IBEW, exemplifies how companies can prepare their workforce for the future while maintaining strong union ties. By aligning union goals with organizational needs, PG&E has ensured that workers remain adaptable to emerging technologies, helping the company stay competitive in an increasingly complex regulatory and operational environment. Similarly, Ford's ability to integrate lean manufacturing principles with union support helped the company navigate difficult financial times, especially during the 2008 financial crisis. This ability to align long-term sustainability with union demands is a key factor in Ford's continued success in a competitive and capital-intensive industry.

5. **Communication and Trust Are Foundational for Productive Labor Relations:** Across these case studies, trust and communication emerge as cornerstones for successful labor relations. Ford's labor–management committees, Kaiser Permanente's LMP, and PG&E's open forums with IBEW, all illustrate that transparent, continuous communication between unions and management leads to more effective conflict resolution and greater workforce engagement. By contrast, the Big Dig's failure to maintain consistent communication and establish fair policies resulted in labor disputes, inefficiency, and significant project overruns.

   These examples demonstrate that trust-building requires consistent effort and that establishing open communication channels early on can prevent small issues from becoming larger, more disruptive conflicts. Regular meetings, clear grievance procedures, and mutual respect between management and union representatives are crucial components of this trust-building process.

The Broader Implications for Unionized Labor Management

The case studies presented here illustrate a number of broader implications for industries that rely on unionized skilled labor. First and foremost, successful organizations recognize that unions are not adversaries but partners in achieving shared goals. Whether it is enhancing safety protocols, preparing for technological shifts, or improving operational efficiency, unions can be valuable collaborators when management engages them early and often in the decision-making process.

Furthermore, industries that fail to prioritize worker engagement, training, and safety will likely face significant operational challenges. The Big Dig Project stands as a cautionary tale of what can happen when labor relations are poorly managed. Delays, cost overruns, safety issues, and employee dissatisfaction are often the result of fragmented or adversarial labor–management dynamics. In contrast, Ford, Kaiser Permanente, and PG&E demonstrate how strong labor–management partnerships lead to better outcomes for workers, the company, and the public.

In addition, these case studies highlight the increasing importance of adaptability. As industries evolve, particularly with the rise of automation, renewable energy, and digitization, companies must invest in their workforce to keep pace with change. Collaborating with unions to provide training and support workers' needs to adapt to these changes ensures both the company's competitiveness and the workers' job security, creating a more sustainable and resilient organization.

Lastly from these case studies, it is clear that the management of unionized skilled labor is not without its challenges, but when approached with a spirit of collaboration, transparency, and mutual respect, it can lead to extraordinary outcomes. Whether in healthcare, utilities, manufacturing, or construction, labor–management partnerships that focus on communication, safety, and continuous improvement create a foundation for long-term success. The lessons learned from Ford, the Big Dig, Kaiser Permanente, and PG&E provide valuable guidance for any organization looking to build stronger, more effective relationships with their unionized workforce.

Conclusion: Lessons Learned and Preparing for the Future

The case studies of Ford Motor Company, the Big Dig, Kaiser Permanente, and PG&E offer a comprehensive view of the critical factors in successfully managing unionized skilled labor. Across industries, these examples illustrate how collaborative labor–management relationships, proactive investment in employee development, prioritization of safety, adaptability to industry shifts, and robust communication strategies form the foundation of productive union partnerships.

These insights reinforce that unions can serve as valuable allies when management engages with them constructively and inclusively. Whether navigating economic downturns, technological advancements, or safety concerns, companies that foster mutual trust, respect, and shared objectives are better equipped to sustain growth and operational resilience.

As we look toward the future, the evolving dynamics of work—including the rise of technology, AI, and automation—will undoubtedly impact the nature of unionized labor. The next chapter delves into how unions and organizations alike are preparing for this shift, examining the role of technology and emerging work structures in shaping the future of union–management relations. Through an exploration of these trends, we'll discuss how management and unions can adapt to continue fostering meaningful partnerships in an increasingly digital world.

CHAPTER 11

The Future of Unions: Technology, AI, and Evolving Work Dynamics

It is one of the characteristics of a free and democratic nation that it have free and independent labor unions.

—Franklin D. Roosevelt

As we look to the future, the role of unions in the workplace will continue to evolve amid the rapid expansion of *artificial intelligence (AI)*, *automation*, and *digitalization*. For *business leaders*, *HR professionals*, union representatives, and *policymakers*, understanding how AI, automation, and digitalization are reshaping the workforce is critical. As industries integrate AI into operations, the landscape of skilled and unskilled labor is changing, requiring a proactive approach to managing the evolving dynamics of employment and labor relations. Whether you are leading a unionized workforce, navigating CBAs, or making strategic decisions on workforce development, this chapter explores the challenges and opportunities AI presents and offers strategies to ensure a fair, equitable, and sustainable future for labor.

As we look ahead, unions must adapt to rapid technological advancements while continuing to protect worker rights. AI-driven automation is not only improving efficiency and productivity but is also eliminating or transforming traditional roles, making retraining, reskilling, and worker protections more important than ever. Studies suggest that nearly 50 percent of tasks currently performed by workers could be automated using existing AI and machine learning technologies, disproportionately impacting low-wage and repetitive jobs in industries such as manufacturing, logistics, and customer service (Brynjolfsson and McAfee 2014, 72).

Meanwhile, AI-enhanced automation is also changing skilled labor markets, increasing demand for digital literacy and hybrid job roles that blend technical expertise with problem-solving capabilities (Acemoglu and Restrepo 2020, 15).

The emergence of AI in unionized workplaces also raises concerns about worker surveillance, job displacement, and bargaining power. Some unions have already begun advocating for policies that regulate AI usage, ensuring that automation enhances rather than replaces human labor (Manyika et al. 2017, 95). Labor organizations and policymakers must work together to address these challenges by establishing clear guidelines on ethical AI deployment, wage protections, and access to upskilling initiatives that prepare workers for AI-driven transformations (Gilewski 2024, 112).

Technological Advancements and Their Impact

AI is no longer an abstract concept—it is already transforming workplaces, redefining job responsibilities, and altering traditional labor structures. Automation is replacing repetitive, manual tasks at an unprecedented rate, increasing efficiency while simultaneously threatening job security. Research indicates that automation could replace as much as 30 percent of global work hours by 2030, affecting millions of workers worldwide (Manyika et al. 2017, 105). Industries that rely on highly structured, predictable tasks, such as manufacturing, logistics, and food services, are especially vulnerable to workforce reductions due to AI integration.

As AI systems take over these roles, unions must advocate for retraining and reskilling programs that help displaced workers transition into new jobs. Collaboration with educational institutions and policymakers is essential in developing certification programs in emerging fields such as AI maintenance, robotics programming, and cybersecurity (Acemoglu and Restrepo 2020, 27). By taking a proactive stance, unions can ensure that automation is implemented as a complement to human labor rather than as a replacement.

Just to make it interesting I prompted AI ChatGPT to make an image of AI, Unions, and Skilled Labor and here is what it created (Figure 11.1):

Figure 11.1 ChatGPT image of AI, unions, and skilled labor

The illustration reflects the collaboration between advanced AI technology and skilled workers in a realistic, slightly futuristic scene. *As you can see on the left there are over two dozen people; and, on the right, there are two people, two robots, and an AI Learning Machine. This should be concerning for union members.*

The use of AI in labor is not without trade-offs. AI improves efficiency, enhances workplace safety, and creates new high-tech employment opportunities, but it also presents risks such as job displacement, wage suppression, and heightened worker surveillance. While predictive maintenance in manufacturing and automated diagnostics in healthcare allow workers to focus on higher-value tasks, these same technologies reduce the need for traditional manual labor. Similarly, AI-driven monitoring systems in warehouses and corporate offices have raised concerns about privacy violations, stress, and unfair performance evaluations (Manyika et al. 2017, 101). If unchecked, AI's role in labor relations could undermine worker autonomy and erode the foundations of collective bargaining.

AI's Impact on Skilled Labor—Transformation, Not Elimination

For skilled workers—such as engineers, technicians, and electricians—AI presents a unique set of opportunities and challenges. Unlike unskilled laborers, who are often at risk of complete job displacement, skilled professionals are more likely to see their job functions evolve rather than disappear.

AI-powered tools assist skilled professionals by improving accuracy, streamlining complex tasks, and reducing workplace hazards. In high-risk industries such as manufacturing, utilities, and construction, AI-powered predictive systems detect equipment failures before they occur, minimizing workplace injuries and fatalities. Smart sensors, automated monitoring systems, and real-time analytics are enabling workers to focus on higher-order problem-solving while allowing AI to handle repetitive or dangerous operations (Acemoglu and Restrepo 2020, 29).

In addition to improving safety, AI is reshaping career progression by creating new roles in automation oversight, cybersecurity, and AI-assisted design. Engineers now use AI-powered simulations to identify design flaws more efficiently, while AI-assisted diagnostic tools help doctors make faster and more accurate medical assessments. Skilled professionals who embrace AI as a tool for augmentation rather than replacement will have greater job security in the evolving labor market.

However, AI introduces concerns that skilled labor cannot afford to ignore. One pressing issue is wage stagnation—as AI increases productivity, fewer workers are needed to produce the same output, reducing employers' incentive to raise wages (Brynjolfsson and McAfee 2014, 78). Another major issue is AI-driven workplace surveillance. Many companies are adopting AI to monitor worker performance in real-time, tracking output, efficiency, and even biometric data. While these systems can improve operational insights, they raise serious privacy concerns and may lead to an unhealthy work environment.

AI's Impact on Unskilled Labor—The Displacement Crisis

For unskilled laborers—such as warehouse workers, cashiers, and assembly-line operators—AI presents a far more immediate risk. Unlike skilled labor, where AI acts as an assistant, many unskilled roles involve repetitive, manual tasks that can be fully automated.

Retail stores are increasingly relying on self-checkout machines, reducing the need for cashiers. In warehouses, robotic sorters powered by AI handle inventory management at speeds and accuracy levels unmatched by human workers. In the fast-food industry, AI-powered kiosks and robotic kitchen assistants are replacing frontline service and food preparation roles.

The benefits of AI in these areas are undeniable—companies experience increased efficiency, lower operational costs, and improved accuracy. Workplace safety also improves as AI reduces the need for humans to engage in physically demanding or hazardous work.

Yet these advancements come at a cost. Mass job displacement is one of the most pressing concerns, as unskilled workers find fewer and fewer employment opportunities in AI-driven workplaces. AI-powered gig work platforms exacerbate this instability, creating on-demand workforces with little to no job security (Gilewski 2024, 127). The rise of algorithmic management means workers are subject to AI-controlled scheduling, pay fluctuations, and job assignments, making it difficult to predict earnings or maintain stable employment.

Beyond displacement, AI surveillance in unskilled jobs raises ethical concerns. Facial recognition, keystroke monitoring, and real-time productivity tracking create high-stress, high-surveillance work environments, leading to mental health concerns and worker dissatisfaction (Manyika et al. 2017, 101).

The Role of Unions in the AI Era

AI is not a distant challenge—it is already reshaping labor, and unions must act now to secure worker protections in this new landscape. Several strategies will be critical to ensuring that AI is used ethically and equitably.

One of the most urgent priorities is collective bargaining for AI-resistant job security. Unions must push for contractual protections that prevent excessive automation, establish worker retraining programs, and ensure that AI-driven productivity gains benefit employees as well as employers.

Reskilling initiatives will also play a vital role in preventing large-scale displacement. Unions must partner with businesses, educational institutions, and government agencies to create training programs that equip workers with the skills needed to transition into AI-enhanced roles.

At the same time, AI-driven workplace surveillance must be regulated. AI should enhance productivity, and not create a punitive, high-pressure environment. Unions should advocate for clear guidelines on AI monitoring, ensuring that it does not infringe on worker autonomy, privacy, or job satisfaction.

Unions must also address the rise of AI-driven gig work. Without proper regulations, AI will continue to undermine traditional employment protections, leaving workers vulnerable to low wages, unpredictable schedules, and reduced benefits. Ensuring portable benefits, fair pay structures, and algorithmic transparency will be essential to protecting workers in the gig economy.

Conclusion

The rise of AI and automation is reshaping labor markets at an unprecedented pace, presenting both opportunities and challenges for unions and the workers they represent. While AI has the potential to enhance productivity, improve workplace safety, and create new job categories, it also poses significant risks, particularly for unskilled laborers whose roles are more susceptible to displacement. Skilled workers may see their roles evolve rather than disappear, but the need for continuous upskilling, ethical AI deployment, and fair labor policies will be critical to ensuring that technological progress does not come at the expense of worker rights.

Unions will play a crucial role in shaping this future, not just by advocating for worker protections and retraining programs, but by ensuring that AI is leveraged as a tool for economic empowerment rather than exploitation. Through collective bargaining, policy advocacy, and strategic partnerships with businesses and educational institutions, unions can help define a future where technological advancements and worker rights coexist. The challenge now lies in navigating these transformations while preserving the core values of labor representation—equity, job security, and fair wages.

Beyond technological shifts, the role of unions extends into broader social and economic spheres. As AI continues to alter employment landscapes, it is essential to examine the wider influence of unions on economic stability, income equality, and workforce development. The accompanying table at the end of this chapter visually summarizes the distinct impacts AI has across unionized workforces, skilled labor, and unskilled roles (Table 11.1). This visual serves as a quick-reference guide, underscoring both the unique challenges and emergent opportunities that AI brings to each sector, and helps illustrate how unions can best navigate the nuanced landscape of tomorrow's workforce. The next chapter will explore the social and economic impact of unions, analyzing how they contribute to wage growth, job security, workforce mobility, and social equity, and how these contributions will be affected by the changing nature of work.

Table 11.1 AI's Impact on unions and skilled and unskilled labor

AI impact	Unions	Skilled labor	Unskilled labor
Job Displacement	AI may automate repetitive tasks, reducing demand for unionized roles in certain sectors.	Specialized skills in decision-making roles are less vulnerable to automation.	Unskilled tasks in retail and warehousing face high displacement risks.
Job Creation	New roles may emerge around AI maintenance, retraining, and support.	Roles may evolve to include AI monitoring and oversight.	Opportunities may arise in basic AI support, though retraining will be critical.
Skill Requirements	Unions can advocate for advanced digital and AI skills training.	Continuous learning in data analytics, machine learning, and AI processes.	Basic tech literacy is needed to adapt to AI-enhanced roles.

(continued)

Table 11.1 AI's Impact on unions and skilled and unskilled labor (continued)

AI impact	Unions	Skilled labor	Unskilled labor
Collective Bargaining	Shift toward negotiating retraining, privacy protections, and job stability.	Emphasis on fair wages reflective of AI-boosted productivity.	Push for stable wages and less invasive AI surveillance.
Workplace Monitoring	Advocate for ethical use and transparency in AI-driven surveillance.	Balance productivity with worker autonomy and data use.	Limit excessive productivity monitoring that reduces autonomy.
Wage Impacts	Advocate for equitable wage sharing from AI-driven productivity.	Potential for wage increases tied to productivity gains from AI.	Address wage pressures from job volatility and displacement.
Training Needs	Push for formal retraining programs and industry certifications.	Advanced certifications and skill updates are needed regularly.	Retraining in AI-driven systems for manual or basic tech tasks.

CHAPTER 12

The Social and Economic Impact of Unions

The union is the true medium of progress, the standard-bearer of human dignity, and the best guarantor of a fair and just society. Where free unions flourish, economic justice and the rights of the people are secure.

—John L. Lewis

Unions are cornerstones of economic justice and social progress, shaping labor conditions far beyond the workplace. Though widely recognized for their role in securing fair wages and benefits, their broader influence extends into economic equality, workplace safety, and national labor policy. At a time when income disparity is widening, automation is disrupting industries, and labor protections face increasing challenges, understanding the economic and social contributions of unions is more critical than ever. Whether through raising wage standards, advocating for safety regulations, or fighting for civil rights, unions play an essential role in shaping a fair and just economy.

Unions and Income Inequality

One of the most notable economic impacts of unions is their role in reducing income inequality. Unions significantly reduce income inequality by establishing higher wage standards that benefit both union and nonunion workers. Research shows that union presence raises wages across entire industries, as nonunion employers often increase pay to prevent unionization—a phenomenon known as the "union threat effect" (Card 2001). This broader impact ensures that even workers outside unionized workplaces experience wage growth, fostering greater economic fairness and stability.

Additionally, the positive economic impact of union-negotiated wages extends beyond individual workers. Higher earnings lead to increased consumer spending, stronger local economies, and more stable communities, reinforcing the broader benefits of a unionized workforce.

Wage Increases

Unions significantly reduce income inequality by establishing higher wage standards that benefit both union and nonunion workers. Research shows that union presence raises wages across entire industries, as non-union employers increase pay to prevent unionization—a phenomenon known as the "union threat effect" (Card 2001). This impact ensures that even workers outside unionized workplaces experience wage growth, contributing to greater economic fairness and stability.

Beyond individual workers, higher wages translate into stronger consumer spending, more resilient local economies, and reduced reliance on social welfare programs, reinforcing the broader economic benefits of a strong unionized workforce.

Benefits and Job Security

Unionized workers often receive better benefits, such as health insurance, retirement plans, and paid leave. These benefits contribute to economic security and help reduce financial stress for workers and their families (Freeman and Medoff 1984). The improved job security that unions provide also gives workers more stability, reducing the uncertainty that many nonunionized employees face. Moreover, the increased predictability in employment that comes with union protection allows families to plan for their futures with greater confidence.

Unions play an instrumental role in advocating for benefits that extend beyond wages. These include protections related to health, family care, and pensions. By negotiating comprehensive benefits, unions help ensure workers are safeguarded against the unforeseen—such as health emergencies—thus providing a critical safety net that minimizes the risk of poverty and financial crisis. In contrast, nonunionized workers are often at the mercy of market conditions, which can lead to uneven and inadequate coverage of essential benefits.

Advocacy for Fair Labor Practices

Unions advocate for policies that promote fair labor practices, such as minimum wage increases and antidiscrimination laws. These policies benefit all workers, not just union members, by creating a more equitable labor market (Hirsch 2004). This broader advocacy helps improve the quality of life for countless individuals and sets a higher standard for employment practices. For instance, union support for legislative measures such as the Family and Medical Leave Act (FMLA) has resulted in significant improvements in workplace rights nationwide.

In addition, unions work to dismantle systemic barriers to economic equity, such as wage theft and employer malfeasance. By holding employers accountable and ensuring labor laws are enforced, unions act as a watchdog for all workers, not just those in unionized sectors. This has led to improvements in labor standards and greater awareness of workers' rights.

Promoting Workplace Safety

Unions have been instrumental in advancing workplace safety, ensuring that employers adhere to strict safety regulations and training requirements. The role of unions in workplace safety is multifaceted, encompassing training programs, policy advocacy, and real-time monitoring to reduce accidents and improve working conditions.

Unions have been instrumental in shaping workplace safety laws, particularly in high-risk industries like construction, manufacturing, and energy. Their advocacy directly influenced the passage of the Occupational Safety and Health Act (OSHA), which established federal safety regulations (Katz 2016). By negotiating for hazard assessments, mandatory protective equipment, and compliance training, unions have helped dramatically reduce workplace injuries and fatalities (Baccaro 2017).

Beyond legislation, unions provide specialized safety training tailored to industry-specific hazards. In sectors such as electrical work, mining, and heavy manufacturing, union-backed training programs have lowered accident rates and increased employer compliance (Friedman 2019). Perhaps most importantly, unions serve as watchdogs—conducting site inspections, reporting safety violations, and holding employers accountable for unsafe conditions before they escalate into workplace disasters.

Perhaps one of the most overlooked contributions of unions is their role as watchdogs—monitoring employer compliance with safety regulations. Unions regularly conduct workplace inspections, report safety violations, and hold employers accountable for unsafe conditions before they escalate into workplace disasters.

Safety Training and Education

Unions provide safety training and education programs to their members, ensuring that workers are aware of potential hazards and know how to protect themselves (Katz 2016). By making safety a priority, unions contribute to a culture that values worker health and well-being. Regular workshops and specialized training sessions help workers understand the best practices in safety protocols, and this knowledge ultimately saves lives.

Safety training provided by unions is also tailored to the specific needs of different industries. For example, in industries such as construction or mining, unions work to ensure workers understand both common and emerging safety challenges. This proactive approach allows workers to mitigate risks effectively, preventing injuries and fatalities.

Advocacy for Safety Regulations

Unions advocate for stronger safety regulations and enforcement, which helps to create safer work environments. This includes lobbying for laws that protect workers from hazardous conditions and holding employers accountable for safety violations (Baccaro 2017). Such advocacy has been instrumental in establishing and maintaining standards that protect worker health. The Occupational Safety and Health Act (OSHA) is a prime example of a regulatory framework that was significantly influenced by union efforts.

Unions' advocacy often extends to demanding transparency in workplace safety reporting. Employers are compelled to maintain accurate records of incidents, and unions use this data to push for corrective actions and improvements in safety standards. This vigilance ensures that employers remain accountable for maintaining safe working conditions and that workers' rights to a safe workplace are respected.

Monitoring and Reporting

Unions often monitor workplace conditions and report safety violations to regulatory agencies. This proactive approach helps to identify and address safety issues before they lead to accidents or injuries (Friedman 2019). By acting as watchdogs, unions ensure that employers prioritize safety in their operations. Moreover, union representatives frequently conduct site inspections and safety audits, offering immediate feedback and corrective suggestions to management.

Unions' efforts to document and publicize unsafe working conditions can also pressure employers to adopt better safety technologies and practices. By maintaining detailed logs of workplace incidents, unions help create a database that can be used to advocate for systemic changes in industry safety standards.

Unions as a Stabilizing Force During Economic Crises

Unions can act as a stabilizing force during economic crises, providing support to workers and helping to maintain economic stability. This includes advocating for policies that protect workers and promote economic recovery. Unions play a vital role in cushioning the impact of economic downturns on workers, ensuring that short-term challenges do not result in long-term economic despair.

Job Protection

During economic downturns, unions negotiate for job protection measures, such as layoff protections and furloughs, to help keep workers employed. This helps to reduce unemployment and maintain consumer spending (Freeman and Medoff 1984). By securing job stability, unions contribute to economic resilience during times of uncertainty. These negotiated protections not only keep workers in their jobs but also allow industries to recover more swiftly once economic conditions improve, avoiding the lengthy rehiring processes that can stymie growth.

The job security that unions help negotiate also extends to provisions for severance and compensation in the event of layoffs. By ensuring that workers receive fair severance packages, unions help to maintain a minimum standard of living for displaced workers, mitigating the worst impacts of economic downturns.

Support for Unemployed Workers

Unions provide support to unemployed workers through benefits, job placement services, and retraining programs. This helps workers transition to new jobs and reduces the impact of unemployment on their families (Hirsch 2004). Unions' efforts in retraining and skill development are crucial in ensuring workers remain employable in shifting economic climates. The availability of union-supported retraining programs often enables workers to enter into emerging industries, thereby increasing their adaptability in a rapidly changing job market.

By partnering with government agencies and educational institutions, unions help provide unemployed workers with access to vocational training and career counseling. These programs focus on equipping workers with skills that are in high demand, such as technology certifications or advanced manufacturing skills, making it easier for them to reenter the workforce.

Advocacy for Economic Policies

Unions advocate for economic policies that promote recovery and growth, such as stimulus packages, infrastructure investments, and social safety nets. These policies help to stabilize the economy and support workers during times of crisis (Card 2001). Unions' political engagement is critical in shaping policies that benefit both workers and the broader economy. For example, union lobbying has often been crucial in pushing for unemployment insurance enhancements during recessions, which have provided vital financial support to millions of households.

The role of unions in advocating for economic stimulus measures ensures that recovery efforts are directed toward not only businesses but also the workers who are integral to economic productivity. Infrastructure projects, often supported by union lobbying, provide critical jobs that stimulate economic growth, further solidifying unions' role as a stabilizing economic force.

Broader Social Justice Impacts

Beyond their economic contributions, unions also play a vital role in promoting broader social justice issues. This includes advocating for civil rights, gender equality, and immigrant rights. Through their commitment to social justice, unions amplify the voices of marginalized communities, fostering inclusion and reducing inequalities.

Civil Rights Advocacy

Unions have a long history of supporting civil rights movements and advocating for equal treatment under the law. This includes fighting against racial discrimination and promoting policies that ensure equal opportunities for all workers (Moody 1988). By standing for social justice, unions extend their influence beyond the workplace into the broader community. The involvement of unions in historical movements such as the Civil Rights Movement of the 1960s demonstrates their broader societal influence.

Unions also advocate for policies that address racial disparities in employment, such as promoting affirmative action in hiring practices. By ensuring that employers uphold principles of nondiscrimination, unions contribute to a more equitable labor market and help dismantle institutional barriers faced by marginalized groups.

Gender Equality

Unions advocate for gender equality in the workplace, including equal pay for equal work, maternity and paternity leave, and protections against sexual harassment. These efforts help to create more inclusive and equitable work environments (Freeman and Medoff 1984). Through collective bargaining and political lobbying, unions have been able to secure key rights for women in the workforce. Union contracts often include provisions for maternity leave, ensuring that women do not have to choose between their careers and family responsibilities.

In addition to workplace protections, unions support initiatives that encourage women to enter traditionally male-dominated fields, such as construction and manufacturing. By promoting educational programs and apprenticeships for women, unions work toward breaking down gender barriers and fostering diversity within various industries.

Unions have a critical role to play in addressing racial and gender inequality in the workplace. By advocating for diversity, equity, and inclusion, unions can help create fair and just work environments. For unions to remain relevant, they must address the specific needs of underrepresented groups in the workforce, ensuring that everyone benefits from technological and economic progress (Brynjolfsson and McAfee 2014). For example, the image below became synonymous with the gender labor movement—"Rosie" published on Norman Rockwell's *Rosie the Riveter* magazine cover (Figure 12.1).

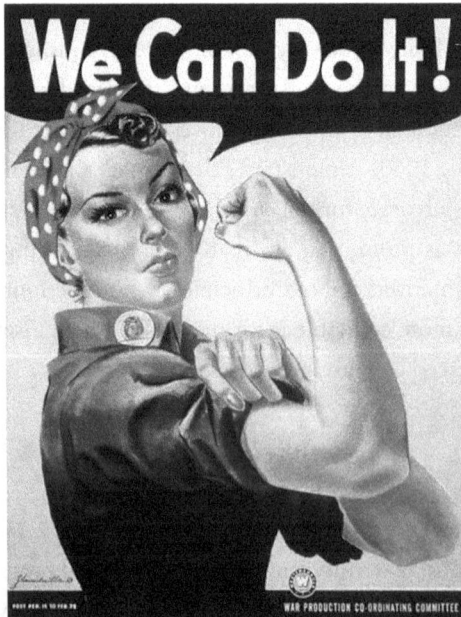

Figure 12.1 Propaganda poster for Westinghouse Electric

Immigrant Rights

Unions support the rights of immigrant workers, advocating for fair treatment and protection from exploitation. This includes lobbying for policies that provide a path to citizenship and ensure that all workers, regardless of their immigration status, are treated with dignity and respect (Baccaro 2017). Unions' support for immigrant rights is crucial for building a diverse and equitable labor force. By organizing immigrant workers and providing them with a platform to voice their concerns, unions help integrate immigrants into the labor market, contributing to social cohesion.

Union-led campaigns against wage theft and workplace abuses that disproportionately affect immigrant workers also highlight the role of unions in ensuring fair treatment for all. By standing up for the most vulnerable workers, unions help to raise labor standards across industries and combat exploitative practices.

Conclusion

The social and economic impact of unions is profound, extending far beyond the workplace. By advocating for fair wages, workplace safety, economic stability, and broader social justice, unions contribute to a more equitable and just society. Their efforts to reduce income inequality, promote safety, stabilize the economy during crises, and to support civil rights, gender equality, and immigrant rights have lasting benefits for all workers and the broader community. The continued relevance and effectiveness of unions depend on their ability to adapt to changing economic conditions and labor markets while remaining steadfast in their commitment to advocating for the rights and well-being of all workers.

As this discussion on unions concludes, one thing is clear: Unions are not relics of the past but vital institutions shaping the future of labor and economic justice. Beyond collective bargaining, unions play a transformative role in reducing income inequality, ensuring workplace safety, and promoting social justice. Their ability to adapt to new economic realities, technological disruptions, and evolving labor structures will determine their continued relevance in shaping fair and just work environments.

The influence of unions extends far beyond wages and contracts—they are pillars of economic fairness, workforce stability, and social justice. As automation, AI, and globalization reshape the labor market, unions must adapt and innovate to ensure that technological progress does not come at the expense of worker protections, fair wages, and job security.

The future of work will not be defined by whether unions exist, but by how they evolve. Will unions harness technology to empower workers, or will automation erode labor rights? Will economic progress be shared among all workers, or will it only benefit the privileged few? The answers to these questions depend on the continued strength, adaptability, and advocacy of unions. The labor movement's legacy will not be measured solely in contracts signed, but in its ability to uphold economic justice, protect human dignity, and champion fair work environments for future generations.

Book Conclusion

In an era of rapid technological advancements, evolving workforce dynamics, and increasingly complex labor relations, managing unionized labor, whether skilled or unskilled, requires more than simply following procedures. It demands strategic foresight, adaptability, and a deep understanding of both historical labor movements and modern workforce challenges.

This book has explored the many dimensions of union management, from the history and cultural foundations of organized labor to the complexities of collective bargaining, workforce safety, and the evolving role of automation and AI. Each chapter has reinforced a central truth: Effective union management is not about control—it is about collaboration. Leaders who approach labor relations with empathy, transparency, and a commitment to fairness are better equipped to build trust, increase productivity, and create resilient, future-ready workplaces.

At its core, successful union management is about building connections—between history and progress, between organizational goals and workers' rights, and between operational efficiency and human dignity. Leaders who respect and empower both skilled and unskilled workers create stronger, more sustainable workplaces that can navigate industry shifts and drive long-term success. When management and labor work together with mutual respect and a shared sense of purpose, they lay the foundation for truly equitable and inclusive workplaces.

As you move into the practical section, "Key Takeaways for Effective Management," let this book serve as both a guide and a call to action. Your leadership plays a critical role in shaping the future of labor relations. By applying the strategies and insights shared here, you will be equipped to lead with integrity, foster meaningful collaboration, and help create a workforce that thrives in both stability and progress. The most successful leaders are not just managers of workers. They are stewards of change, builders of trust, and champions of a more inclusive and prosperous future for workers and organizations alike.

PART 4

Conclusion and Additional Resources

Key Takeaways
for Effective Management

Managing unionized labor effectively requires a blend of strategic adaptability, empathetic leadership, and a commitment to fair, collaborative practices. Here are the central takeaways that encapsulate the core lessons from *Leading Unionized Workforces in the Age of AI: Managing Skilled and Unskilled Labor in a Changing World:*

1. **Foster Collaborative Relationships with Union Representatives**
   Establishing trust and a spirit of collaboration with union representatives is foundational. Proactive engagement with unions helps anticipate and address challenges and creates a partnership that balances organizational goals with labor interests (Freeman and Medoff 1984). Consistent communication and joint decision making build credibility and facilitate smoother conflict resolution.

2. **Promote Transparent, Fair, and Consistent Policies**
   Clear, equitable policies foster trust and enhance morale. Implementing uniform standards in areas such as job descriptions, attendance, and discipline promotes a fair working environment that respects union guidelines (Katz 2016). Consistency in policy application helps to build a foundation of mutual respect between management and the workforce.

3. **Invest in Continuous Learning and Skill Development**
   Training and skill development are critical in helping workers adapt to evolving job demands. Collaborative efforts between management and unions to develop relevant training programs not only enhance productivity but also signal an investment in employees' growth (Brynjolfsson and McAfee 2014). By focusing on continuous learning, managers can create a workforce that remains resilient and competitive.

4. **Make Workplace Safety a Shared Priority**
   Safety is essential in managing unionized labor, particularly in high-risk industries. By partnering with unions on safety initiatives and advocating for regular training and audits, managers foster a safety-conscious culture that prioritizes the well-being of workers (Baccaro 2017). Empowering workers to participate in safety protocols and risk reporting further strengthens this commitment.

5. **Adapt Leadership Style to Match the Work Environment**
   Effective managers tailor their leadership style to fit the unique demands of different environments. From participative approaches in production to coaching and mentoring in more technical roles, adaptability is key (Hirsch 2004). Each unionized environment may require a nuanced approach that emphasizes empathy, fairness, and respect for workers' specific roles and challenges.

6. **Engage in Ethical AI and Technology Integration**
   AI and automation are transforming the labor landscape, bringing both opportunities and disruptions. Managers must be proactive in understanding how AI affects job roles, productivity, and worker security. Collaborating with unions to develop reskilling programs and advocating for ethical AI implementation can help mitigate concerns about job displacement (Gilewski 2024). Negotiating worker protections around AI-driven performance monitoring, privacy, and data usage ensures that technological advancements align with fair labor practices (Manyika et al. 2017). The successful integration of AI depends on balancing operational efficiency with the ethical considerations that uphold worker dignity and autonomy.

7. **Leverage Union Expertise for Social and Economic Impact**
   Beyond the workplace, unions contribute to economic equity, social justice, and workplace rights advocacy. Effective managers recognize the broader role unions play in supporting fair labor practices, safety standards, and societal progress (Friedman 2019). By aligning with these values, managers foster a positive organizational culture that supports broader societal goals, reinforcing the organization's social responsibility and public image.

8. **Prepare for Future Workforce Trends**

   The workforce will continue to evolve with advancements in technology, the rise of the gig economy, and shifting labor regulations. Successful managers must remain adaptable by anticipating these changes and developing long-term workforce strategies. Investing in workforce development, supporting flexible work arrangements, and advocating for inclusive labor policies will ensure that organizations and employees alike remain resilient in the face of transformation (Acemoglu and Restrepo 2020). Future-ready managers not only respond to industry trends but actively shape the workplace of tomorrow.

Final Thoughts on Managing Unionized Employees

The journey of managing unionized labor, whether skilled or unskilled, is as complex as it is rewarding. As explored throughout this book, effective management in unionized environments requires a balance of strategic insight, empathy, and an unwavering commitment to fairness. The role of a manager extends beyond enforcing policy or driving productivity; it involves fostering a culture of respect, collaboration, and shared purpose between labor and management.

Unionized employees, both skilled and unskilled, form the backbone of industries critical to our economy. Skilled workers bring specialized expertise and an inherent understanding of operational complexities, while unskilled workers provide essential support that enables these industries to function effectively. Managing such a diverse workforce is not just about ensuring tasks are completed or safety protocols are followed—it is about creating an environment where all employees feel valued, heard, and supported. A collaborative relationship with unions, underpinned by open communication, transparency, and mutual respect, is vital to achieving this goal.

As industries evolve with advancements in AI, digitalization, and shifting labor dynamics, managers face increasing pressure to navigate these transformations thoughtfully. The integration of AI and automation not only promises enhanced efficiency but also raises critical questions about job security, workers' rights, and ethical considerations. Rather than viewing these changes as disruptions, managers should embrace them as opportunities to partner with unions in advocating for reskilling initiatives and redefining job roles to align with the needs of a modern workforce. By adopting a responsible approach to technology that safeguards the dignity and autonomy of all employees, leaders can help shape a workplace that thrives in this era of rapid change.

Unions have long played a transformative role in advocating for workers' rights, social justice, and equity. Today, they continue to champion critical issues such as income equality, workplace safety, and inclusivity. Effective managers recognize that these values are foundational to creating stable, fair, and prosperous workplaces. By aligning management practices with the principles of fairness and inclusivity, organizations are better equipped to thrive in an increasingly diverse and interconnected world.

Ultimately, the art of managing unionized labor lies in understanding that people are the most valuable asset of any organization. Managers who respect this reality and approach labor relations as a partnership will cultivate a resilient workforce capable of adapting to change, meeting challenges head-on, and driving sustained success. Within this dynamic and ever-evolving relationship lies the greatest opportunity for managers to lead not just for today but also for the future.

As the labor landscape continues to transform, let this book serve as a guide, a reminder, and a source of inspiration for managers seeking to navigate the complexities of unionized workforces with skill, respect, and integrity. May each management decision be driven by a commitment to honor the human side of labor, bridging the gap between organizational goals and the aspirations of the individuals who bring them to life.

Encouragement
for Continuous Learning
and Adaptation

In a rapidly changing world, the skills and strategies that make an effective manager today will inevitably need to evolve. Managing unionized skilled labor is a nuanced and dynamic role that requires a commitment to continuous learning, adaptability, and open-mindedness. By embracing change, managers can stay aligned with both the needs of their workforce and the demands of their industry.

Continuous learning is not merely an exercise in keeping up with new regulations or technologies; it is a pathway to deepening understanding, gaining new perspectives, and refining one's approach to leadership. Whether it is participating in labor relations workshops, seeking insights on AI's evolving role in the workforce, or exploring ways to improve safety protocols, each opportunity to learn strengthens the manager's capacity to lead effectively.

Adaptation is equally essential. The landscape of unionized labor is changing rapidly, with advancements in automation, AI, and shifts toward remote work fundamentally transforming the nature of many skilled roles. Managers must be prepared to navigate these changes thoughtfully, working alongside unions to ensure that technological integration benefits employees and respects the principles of fairness, transparency, and respect. This flexibility will empower managers to handle change proactively, making decisions that safeguard both the interests of their workforce and the long-term health of the organization.

For managers of unionized skilled labor, staying current on labor law, emerging technologies, and effective communication strategies can be the difference between fostering a productive work environment and facing preventable challenges. Equipping oneself with the latest knowledge and best practices is an investment in not only one's career but also in the success and well-being of every team member.

In closing, let this book serve as a foundation for continuous growth, a reminder that effective management is a journey rather than a destination. By fostering a mindset of curiosity, resilience, and adaptability, managers can rise to meet the challenges of tomorrow while honoring the principles of respect and collaboration that underpin successful labor relations today. Remember, the journey of learning is a lifelong commitment—one that will empower you to lead with confidence, inspire those around you, and shape a more equitable, productive, and thriving workplace.

Appendixes

APPENDIX A

Key Terms and Definitions

This glossary includes essential terms used throughout the book to assist readers in understanding critical concepts related to unionized labor.

- **Collective Bargaining Agreement (CBA)**: A contract negotiated between union representatives and employers that outlines wages, hours, benefits, and working conditions for union members.
- **Grievance Procedure**: A formal process outlined in CBAs for addressing and resolving disputes between union members and management.
- **Labor Union**: An organized group of workers formed to protect and advance their rights and interests, often focused on wages, benefits, and working conditions.
- **Automation and AI in Labor**: Technologies designed to streamline or replace human tasks, impacting productivity, job roles, and workplace dynamics.
- **Workplace Safety Protocols**: Standards and practices established to ensure worker safety, often negotiated in union agreements.

APPENDIX B

Sample Union Contract Clauses

This section provides sample language for core contract clauses, illustrating typical terms in unionized environments.

- **Wage and Benefit Provisions**: Example language establishing pay scales, overtime, and health benefits.
- **Safety and Health Provisions**: Sample clauses outlining safety measures, employer obligations, and training requirements.
- **Training and Apprenticeship Provisions**: Language detailing joint union–management training initiatives and certification pathways.
- **Grievance Procedures**: Step-by-step process language for handling grievances, from initial filing to final arbitration.

APPENDIX C

Tools for Effective Management of Unionized Skilled Labor

These practical tools support managers in maintaining positive labor relations and improving workplace communication.

1. **Union Relations Checklist**: A checklist of proactive communication practices, meeting strategies, and relationship-building tips.
2. **Grievance Tracking Template**: A structured template for logging and tracking grievances, including fields for description, resolution steps, timeline, and outcomes.
3. **Employee Engagement Survey**: A customizable survey template focused on assessing engagement, satisfaction, safety, and training for unionized workers.

APPENDIX D

Case Studies—Additional Insights

This section provides supplemental summaries of real-world case studies for deeper exploration.

1. **Success with Collaborative AI Integration in a Unionized Manufacturing Environment**
2. **Challenges in Implementing Safety Protocols: Lessons from High-Risk Industries**
3. **Effective Crisis Management with Union Partnerships during Economic Downturns**

Each case study provides insights into unique challenges, strategies, and outcomes of union–management collaboration.

APPENDIX E

Reference Tables and Figures

This appendix includes key tables and figures for quick reference, offering visual summaries of concepts discussed in the book.

1. **Leadership Styles by Union Type Table**: A breakdown of recommended leadership approaches (e.g., Transformational, Participative) for each type of union.
2. **Impact of AI on Unionized Labor Table**: A summary table showing AI's varying effects on unions, skilled labor, and unskilled labor across dimensions like job displacement, wage impacts, and skill requirements.
3. **Historical Timeline of Labor Unions and Legislation**: A timeline illustrating major union milestones, significant strikes, and legislative changes.

APPENDIX F

Recommended Reading and Resources

For readers interested in diving deeper, this appendix lists books, articles, and online resources relevant to managing unionized labor.

- **Books on Labor Relations**: *What Do Unions Do?* by Freeman and Medoff; *The Second Machine Age* by Brynjolfsson and McAfee.
- **Articles on AI and Labor**: Research articles exploring the impact of automation and AI on labor dynamics.
- **Government and Union Resources**: Links to websites for major unions, Department of Labor resources, and labor rights organizations.

Frequently Asked Questions (FAQs)

A collection of frequently asked questions to address practical management concerns in unionized settings.

- **How should I approach contract negotiations as a new manager in a unionized environment?**
- **What are best practices for managing grievances efficiently?**
- **How can I navigate conflicts between union goals and company goals?**

Each question provides concise, actionable responses to guide managers in handling complex union-related situations.

APPENDIX H

Sample Training Modules for Managers

Suggested training modules to help managers develop the skills needed for effective union management.

1. **Collective Bargaining Basics**: Objectives, suggested activities, and takeaways for understanding CBAs and negotiation tactics.
2. **Effective Communication with Union Representatives**: Best practices for maintaining respectful and open communication channels.
3. **AI and Technology in Unionized Workplaces**: An overview of how to responsibly introduce technology in unionized settings, including privacy and job transition strategies.

APPENDIX I

Sample Collective Bargaining Agreements

Article 1: Recognition

The employer recognizes the union as the exclusive representative of all employees covered by this agreement for the purpose of collective bargaining with respect to wages, hours, and other terms and conditions of employment.

Article 2: Management Rights

The employer retains the exclusive right to manage the business, including the right to hire, promote, discipline, and discharge employees, subject to the terms of this agreement.

Article 3: Wages

The employer agrees to pay employees in accordance with the wage schedule attached to this agreement. Any changes to the wage schedule shall be negotiated with the union.

Article 4: Hours of Work

The standard workweek shall consist of 40 hours, Monday through Friday. Overtime shall be paid at the rate of 1.5 times the regular hourly rate for all hours worked beyond 40 hours in a workweek.

Article 5: Grievance Procedure

Employees who believe that their rights under this agreement have been violated may file a grievance with the union. The grievance shall be processed in accordance with the following steps: Step 1: Informal discussion with the immediate supervisor; Step 2: Written grievance submitted to the department head; Step 3: Grievance meeting with union and employer representatives; and Step 4: Arbitration.

Article 6: Safety and Health

The employer agrees to provide a safe and healthy work environment and to comply with all applicable safety and health regulations. The union shall have the right to participate in safety inspections and to raise safety concerns with the employer.

Article 7: Training and Development

The employer agrees to provide training and development opportunities for employees to enhance their skills and advance their careers. The union and employer shall work together to identify training needs and develop training programs.

Article 8: Seniority

Seniority shall be determined by the length of continuous service with the employer. In the event of layoffs, promotions, or transfers, seniority shall be the determining factor, provided that the employee has the necessary qualifications and abilities to perform the work.

Article 9: Union Rights

The union shall have the right to hold meetings, distribute literature, and communicate with members on the employer's premises, provided that such activities do not interfere with the normal operations of the business.

Article 10: No Strike/No Lockout

The union agrees not to engage in any strikes, work stoppages, or slow-downs during the term of this agreement. The employer agrees not to lock out employees during the term of this agreement.

Article 11: Duration

This agreement shall be effective from [Start Date] to [End Date]. Either party may request to renegotiate the agreement by providing written notice at least 60 days prior to the expiration date.

Respecting Skilled Labor Expertise in Unionized Environments

Managing unionized skilled labor requires a profound respect for the unique expertise and technical acumen each trade brings to the workplace. Tasks that may appear straightforward often involve layers of safety protocols, technical specifications, and collaborative coordination among various trades. This appendix explores the critical aspects of respecting skilled labor expertise in both unionized and nonunionized environments.

Task Complexity and Safety Requirements

In a unionized setting, even tasks like replacing light bulbs above industrial equipment demand strict adherence to protocols and involve several steps:

- Safety Job Briefing: Identifying potential risks and preventive measures.
- Lockout/Tagout (LOTO): Isolating energy sources to prevent accidental activation.
- Fall Protection: Ensuring appropriate equipment for tasks at height.
- ARC Flash Gear: Using PPE to shield against electrical hazards.
- Environmental Risks: Addressing heat exposure near industrial ovens.

These procedures not only ensure worker safety but also reflect the complexity of task planning in unionized environments where each trade's role is clearly defined and protected.

Union Versus Nonunion Approaches to Skilled Labor

Unionized Approach

In unionized environments, each task is allocated to a specific trade based on established roles and CBAs. For example:

- An electrician may troubleshoot electrical components but will not handle the mechanical disconnection of motors or parts, which is reserved for millwrights.
- A machinist is responsible for precision alignment, while the warehouse team handles inventory and part transport.
- Each trade's involvement is governed by the union contract, meaning supervisors must coordinate with multiple trades and adhere to overtime polling, safety pairings, and trade-specific guidelines.

This structured approach ensures expertise, maintains high safety standards, and minimizes equipment downtime, although it can sometimes extend project timelines due to multi-trade coordination.

Nonunion Approach

In nonunionized settings, skilled labor often adopts a more flexible, "jack-of-all-trades" model. In these environments:

- Workers may be cross-trained, enabling them to complete multiple types of tasks without waiting for specialists. An electrician might troubleshoot, disconnect, and align a motor, completing the job independently.
- Supervisors can assign tasks based on availability and urgency rather than specific trade roles, potentially accelerating task completion.

- Safety protocols are still followed (e.g., LOTO, fall protection) but may be less prescriptive in terms of trade involvement and role-specific requirements.

While the nonunion approach can lead to faster task completion and reduce labor costs, it may also lack the rigorous safety oversight and specialized expertise that unionized environments enforce.

Supervising a Skilled Labor Task: Detailed Scenario

Consider a scenario involving a critical motor failure that requires immediate attention. In a unionized setting, supervisors coordinate with electricians for troubleshooting, millwrights for rigging, and machinists for precision alignment. Overtime polling is required for each trade, and each worker operates within clearly defined roles to ensure compliance with the CBA.

In contrast, in a nonunionized setting, a single skilled worker or a smaller team might handle multiple aspects of the repair, leading to a quicker, more flexible response. However, without the same strict adherence to role delineation, the task might proceed with reduced oversight or risk-specific training, potentially impacting long-term equipment reliability.

Cross-Trade Collaboration: A Practical Example

In unionized settings, a composite crew working on equipment may include multiple trades, each handling their specific duties. For example:

- Electricians handle disconnections and reconnections.
- Millwrights perform rigging and mechanical setup.
- Machinists handle alignment and precision fitting.

In nonunionized settings, a worker might perform all these tasks alone or with minimal support, allowing for quicker resolution but potentially compromising task precision or safety.

Key Takeaways on Respecting Skilled Labor Expertise

1. Adherence to Trade Boundaries in Union Settings: Ensuring each task is managed by the appropriate trade supports safety, efficiency, and compliance with union agreements.
2. Safety Prioritization: Rigorous adherence to protocols in union settings is a critical safeguard but can be adapted with flexibility in nonunion settings.
3. Proactive Planning: In union settings, planning for trade-specific needs is essential to avoid delays and prevent grievances.
4. Collaborative Problem-Solving: Clear communication across trades in unionized settings minimizes misunderstandings and ensures a smooth workflow.

This appendix emphasizes the importance of managing skilled labor expertise respectfully in both unionized and nonunionized settings, highlighting the strengths of each approach while underscoring the unique challenges and advantages in unionized environments.

APPENDIX K

Company B Electrical Apprenticeship Agreement

Electrician Apprenticeship created by Nick E. Gilewski for an operator to become an electrician, which was created on 8/22/2012 1:41 p.m.:

Company B Electrician Apprenticeship

<u>Description</u>

Electricians work in a wide variety of areas within the plant, on everything from lighting, medium voltage (4160v) motor starters, and PLCs.

An electrician's work involves assembling, installing, testing, maintaining, servicing, and operating electrical systems and equipment.

During this apprenticeship, the apprentice will work in the plant under direct supervision of a qualified electrician **at all times**.

The Globe apprenticeship will last a minimum of two (2) years.

At the end of the apprenticeship the apprentice will know:

- Electrical Safety NFPA 70E and National Electric Code
- Basic Electrical Fundamentals
- Meters and Test Equipment
- Electrical Prints and Drawings
- AC Motor Controls
- Electrical Code and Wiring
- Alternating Current Fundamentals
- Single-Phase Alternating Current Circuits
- Circuit Protection Devices

- Single-Phase Transformers
- Alternating Current Motor Controls
- Lighting
- Industrial Power Electronics (PLCs, VFDs)
- Three-Phase Alternating Current Circuits
- Three-Phase Transformers
- Crane Repair
- Brake Adjustments
- Actuator Adjustments and Repair
- Heavy Motor Rigging

Most, if not all of this training will be OJT (On-the-Job Training).

The apprentice will maintain a log of work that they perform every-day, which will be reviewed on the last day of their scheduled shift by the maintenance supervisor or their representative with the apprentice.

A qualified plant electrician will assist in assessing the level of electrical knowledge the apprentice has achieved.

Resources for Further Reading

Books on Labor Relations and Union Management

1. **Freeman, Richard B., and James. L. Medoff. 1984.** *What Do Unions Do?* Basic Books.
   - A classic in labor studies, this book explores the role of unions in improving workplace conditions, wages, and productivity.
2. **Katz, Harry C. 2016.** *Labor Relations in a Globalizing World.* Cornell University Press.
   - An insightful exploration of labor relations with a focus on the global labor market, union dynamics, and evolving employer–employee relationships.
3. **Gould IV, William B. 2022.** *A Primer on American Labor Law.* Cambridge University Press.
   - A comprehensive overview of American labor law, covering major legislation, labor rights, and the legal landscape of unions.
4. **Rosenfeld, Jake. 2014.** *What Unions No Longer Do.* Harvard University Press.
   - This book examines the declining influence of unions in the United States and their changing role in the modern workforce.
5. **Brynjolfsson, Erik, and Andrew McAfee. 2014.** *The Second Machine Age: Work, Progress, and Prosperity in a Time of Brilliant Technologies.* W.W. Norton & Company.
   - A groundbreaking analysis of how technology, including AI, is reshaping labor markets and implications for skilled labor.

Articles on Technology, AI, and Unionized Labor

1. **Acemoglu, Daron, and Pascual Restrepo. 2020.** "The Race between Man and Machine: Implications of Technology for Growth, Factor Shares, and Employment." *American Economic Review* 108 (6): 1488–1542.
   - A critical examination of how technological advancements affect labor, employment, and wage dynamics, with insights into unionized sectors.

2. **De Stefano, Valerio. 2016.** "The Rise of the Just-in-time Workforce: On-Demand Work, Crowdwork, and Labor Protection in the gig Economy." *Comparative Labor Law & Policy Journal* 37: 471.
   - This article explores labor protections in the gig economy and how unions might adapt to new work arrangements.
3. **Hirsch, Barry T. 2004.** "Reconsidering Union Wage Effects: Surveying New Evidence on an Old Topic." *Journal of Labor Research* 25 (2): 233–266.
   - An analysis of the effects of union membership on wage inequality, shedding light on economic outcomes for union and nonunion workers.
4. **Friedman, Gerald. 2019.** "Rethinking Labor Unions: The Role of Union Structure in a Changing Labor Market." *ILR Review* 72 (3): 627–648.
   - A discussion on the structural evolution of unions and strategies for remaining effective in a changing labor market.

Online Resources and Websites

1. **AFL-CIO**—https://aflcio.org
   - The official site of the American Federation of Labor and Congress of Industrial Organizations, which provides resources on labor rights, union history, and current labor issues.
2. **U.S. Department of Labor—Occupational Safety and Health Administration (OSHA)**—https://www.osha.gov
   - OSHA provides comprehensive information on workplace safety standards and regulations, which are essential for unionized workplaces.
3. **National Labor Relations Board (NLRB)**—https://www.nlrb.gov/
   - The NLRB's site offers detailed information on labor laws, workers' rights, and guidance on union organizing and collective bargaining.
4. **McKinsey Global Institute Reports**—https://www.mckinsey.com/mgi
   - This research institute offers insightful reports on technology, automation, and the future of work, valuable for understanding AI's impact on labor markets.
5. **Power for America Training Trust Fund**—https://www.power4america.org
   - An organization that provides training and apprenticeship programs to ensure union workers are prepared for future energy and technology challenges.
6. **National Joint Apprenticeship and Training Committee (NJATC)**—https://www.njatc.org
   - A training organization offering programs and certifications for unionized skilled labor, particularly in the electrical and technical fields.

Recommended Reading on Labor History and Social Impact of Unions

1. **Foner, Philip S. 1980.** *History of the Labor Movement in the United States.* International Publishers.
   - A multivolume series that provides a detailed history of the labor movement, unions, and worker rights in the United States.
2. **Brody, David. 1980.** *Workers in Industrial America: Essays on the Twentieth Century Struggle.* Oxford University Press.
   - This collection of essays explores the history and challenges of industrial workers and the labor movement in America.
3. **Marx, Karl. 1976.** *Capital: Volume I.* Penguin Classics.
   - An influential work on labor, capitalism, and class dynamics, providing foundational perspectives on labor rights and economic equality.
4. **Freeman, Richard B., and James. L. Medoff. 1984.** *What Do Unions Do?* Basic Books.
   - A foundational work examining the role of unions in wage negotiation, workplace conditions, and overall economic impact.

References

Acemoglu, Daron, and Pascual Restrepo. 2018. "Artificial Intelligence, Automation and Work." NBER Working Paper 24196. National Bureau of Economic Research. https://doi.org/10.3386/w24196.

Acemoglu, Daron, and Pascual Restrepo. 2020. "The Race Between Man and Machine: Implications of Technology for Growth, Factor Shares, and Employment." *American Economic Review* 108 (6): 1488–1542.

AFL-CIO. 2022. "Shuler at LAMPAC: The Clean Energy Transition Is Our Generation's Defining Opportunity." *AFL-CIO*, October 3, 2023. https://aflcio.org/speeches/shuler-lampac-clean-energy-transition-our-generations-defining-opportunity.

Avrich, Paul. 1984. *The Haymarket Tragedy*. Princeton University Press.

Baccaro, Luigi. 2017. "The Global Economic and Financial Crisis: Impact on Trade Unions in the European Union." *International Journal of Labour Research* 9 (1): 23–40.

Bakery, Confectionery, Tobacco Workers, and Grain Millers International Union. 2023. "About the BCTGM." https://www.bctgm.org.

Bilginsoy, Cengiz. 2003. "The Hazards of Training: Attrition and Retention in Construction Industry Apprenticeship Programs." *Industrial and Labor Relations Review* 57 (1): 54–67.

Brynjolfsson, Erik, and Andrew McAfee. 2014. *The Second Machine Age: Work, Progress, and Prosperity in a Time of Brilliant Technologies*. W.W. Norton & Company.

Bureau of Labor Statistics. 2022. "Workplace Injury, Illness, and Fatality Statistics." https://www.bls.gov.

California Public Employment Relations Board (PERB). 2023. "The Unfair Practice Charge Process—An Overview." Accessed May 28, 2025. https://perb.ca.gov/how-to-file-an-unfair-practice-charge/the-unfair-practice-charge-process-an-overview/.

Card, David. 2001. "The Effect of Unions on Wage Inequality in the U.S. Labor Market." *Industrial and Labor Relations Review* 54 (2): 296–315.

Constitutional Law Reporter. n.d. "National Labor Relations Act (Wagner Act)." https://constitutionallawreporter.com/2018/01/31/nlra-wagner-act/.

Derickson, Alan. 1988. *Workers' Health, Workers' Democracy: The Western Miners' Struggle, 1891–1925*. Cornell University Press.

De Stefano, Valerio. 2016. "The Rise of the Just-in-Time Workforce: On-Demand Work, Crowdwork, and Labor Protection in the Gig Economy." *Comparative Labor Law & Policy Journal* 37: 471.

Ebbets, Charles C. (Photographer). 1932. "Lunch Atop a Skyscraper." Photograph. Getty Images. https://en.wikipedia.org/wiki/Lunch_atop_a_Skyscraper.

Epstein, Stephan R. 1991. "Craft Guilds, Apprenticeship, and Technological Change in Preindustrial Europe." *Journal of Economic History* 51 (3): 684–713.

Encyclopedia Britannica. n.d. "International Workingmen's Association." https://www.britannica.com/topic/First-International.

Foner, Philip S. 1980. *History of the Labor Movement in the United States: Volume 2*. International Publishers.

Ford Motor Company and United Auto Workers (UAW) Collaboration. 2008. "Navigating Economic Challenges: Ford and UAW Collaboration on Continuous Improvement Programs, Workplace Safety, and Employee Training." *Ford Motor Company Annual Report*. https://www.annualreports.com/HostedData/AnnualReportArchive/f/NYSE_F_2008.pdf.

Freeman, Richard B., and James L. Medoff. 1984. *What Do Unions Do?* Basic Books.

Friedman, Gerald. 2019. "Rethinking Labor Unions: The Role of Union Structure in a Changing Labor Market." *ILR Review* 72 (3): 627–648.

Gilewski, N. E. 2024. *Leading Unionized Workforces in the Age of AI: Managing Skilled and Unskilled Labor in a Changing World*.

Gould IV, William B. 2022. *A Primer on American Labor Law*. Cambridge University Press.

Green, James. 2006. *Death in the Haymarket: A Story of Chicago, the First Labor Movement, and the Bombing That Divided Gilded Age America*. Pantheon.

Gross, James A. 1981. *The Making of the National Labor Relations Board: A Study in Economics, Politics, and the Law*. SUNY Press.

Heery, Edmund, and Mike Noon. 2017. *A Dictionary of Human Resource Management and Labor Relations*. 4th ed. Oxford University Press.

Hirsch, Barry T. 2004. "Reconsidering Union Wage Effects: Surveying New Evidence on an Old Topic." *Journal of Labor Research* 25 (2): 233–266.

Hobsbawm, Eric J. 1964. *Labouring Men: Studies in the History of Labour*. Weidenfeld and Nicolson.

International Association of Machinists and Aerospace Workers. 2023. "About the IAMAW." https://www.goiam.org.

International Brotherhood of Electrical Workers. 2023. "About the IBEW." https://www.ibew.org.

International Union of Operating Engineers. 2023. "About the IUOE." https://www.iuoe.org.

IUOE National Training Fund. 2022. "Apprenticeship and Training." https://www.iuoe.org/training.

Kaiser Permanente. 2019. "Labor Management Partnership: 20 Years of Collaboration and Innovation." https://www.lmpartnership.org/stories/new-book-spotlights-labor-management-partnership-success.

Katz, Harry C., Thomas A. Kochan, and Alexander J.S. Colvin. *An Introduction to U.S. Collective Bargaining and Labor Relations*. 4th ed. Ithaca, NY: Cornell University Press, 2017.

Katz, Harry C. 2016. *Labor Relations in a Globalizing World*. Cornell University Press.

Klein, Melvyn. 2016. *The Pullman Strike and the Power of Organized Labor*. University of Illinois Press.

Krause, Peter. 1992. *The Battle for Homestead, 1880–1892: Politics, Culture, and Steel*. University of Pittsburgh Press.

Levy, Peter. 2018. *The Long Shadow of Labor: Unions, Politics, and the Enduring Tensions of the Postwar Period*. Princeton University Press.

Lindsey, A. 2019. "The Pullman Strike of 1894: Federal Intervention and the Limits of Worker Resistance." *Labor History* 60 (2): 187–202.

Manyika, James, Michael Chui, Mehdi Miremadi, et al. 2017. *A Future That Works: Automation, Employment, and Productivity*. McKinsey Global Institute.

Marwick, Arthur. 1973. *The Deluge: British Society and the First World War*. Pelican Books.

Marx, Karl. 1976. *Capital: Volume I*. Penguin Classics.

Marxists Internet Archive. n.d. "First International (International Workingmen's Association)." https://www.marxists.org/history/international/iwma/index.htm.

Massachusetts Turnpike Authority. 2007. "Final Report on the Central Artery/Tunnel Project (Big Dig)." https://www.mass.gov/lists/oig-central-arterytunnel-cat-big-dig-reports-1994-2007.

McAteer, John D. 2007. *Monongah: The Tragedy of the 1907 Monongah Mine Disaster, the Worst Industrial Accident in U.S. History*. West Virginia University Press.

Moody, Kim. 1988. *An Injury to All: The Decline of American Unionism*. Verso.

Montgomery, David. 1980b. *Workers' Control in America: Studies in the History of Work, Technology, and Labor Struggles*. Cambridge University Press.

National Joint Apprenticeship and Training Committee. 2022. "Training the Future." https://electricaltrainingalliance.org/.

National Labor Relations Board. n.d. "National Labor Relations Act." https://www.nlrb.gov/guidance/key-reference-materials/national-labor-relations-act

NYCOSH. n.d. "Bargaining for Safety and Health." https://nycosh.org/about/.

Pacific Gas and Electric Company. 2022 "Working Together: PG&E and IBEW Partnership for Safety and Excellence." https://ibew1245.com/wp-content/uploads/2022/06/IBEW-Letter-Agreement-Reference-Document.pdf.

Power for America Training Trust Fund. 20232025. "Utility Workers Union of America (UWUA)." https://uwua.net/programs/power-for-america-training-trust-fund/.

Rosenfeld, Jake. 2014. *What Unions No Longer Do*. Harvard University Press.

Scheiber, Noam. 2021. "Kellogg Workers Ratify New Contract and End Nearly Three-Month Strike." *The New York Times*, December 16. https://www .nytimes.com/2021/12/21/business/economy/kellogg-union-strike-contract .html.

Smith, Christopher. 2016. "The Haymarket Affair: America's Bloody Confrontation Between Labor and Capital." *Journal of American History* 102 (4): 984–1012.

State of the Union History. 2017. "1886: Grover Cleveland—Request to Enlarge the Labor Bureau with Power to Arbitrate Disputes." https://www .stateoftheunionhistory.com/2017/09/1886-grover-cleveland-request-to .html.

Strauss, George. 1991. "Union Democracy." *Institute for Research on Labor Employment*. https://irle.berkeley.edu/publications/working-papers/union-democracy/.

United Steelworkers. 2023. "About the USW." https://www.usw.org.

U.S. Department of Labor. n.d. "History of Labor Day." https://www.dol.gov /general/laborday/history.

Utility Workers Union of America. 2023. https://uwua.net.

About the Author

Dr. Nick E. Gilewski is an accomplished engineering manager, adjunct professor, and industry leader with over 25 years of experience managing unionized and nonunionized workforces across manufacturing, utilities, and high-tech industries. His expertise lies at the intersection of leadership, technology, and labor relations, making him a sought-after voice in navigating the evolving workforce landscape shaped by artificial intelligence and automation.

Dr. Gilewski holds a doctoral degree from Niagara University and advanced degrees in industrial engineering and business administration, equipping him with a robust foundation in both the technical and managerial aspects of his field. His professional credentials include certifications as a Six Sigma Green Belt, Project Management Professional (PMP), Certified Maintenance and Reliability Professional (CMRP), and Associate Certified Coach (ACC)—demonstrating his deep commitment to operational efficiency, continuous improvement, and workforce optimization.

With experience leading teams through technological transitions, AI-driven automation, and workforce restructuring, Dr. Gilewski has developed strategies to help organizations integrate emerging technologies while preserving job security, upskilling workers, and fostering labor–management collaboration. His expertise extends to cross-functional leadership, project execution, electrical engineering system upgrades, lean manufacturing, and data-driven decision making.

Currently serving as an Executive Engineering Manager at Samsung Semiconductor Manufacturing in Austin, Texas, Dr. Gilewski spearheads initiatives in high-stakes production environments where automation and AI are transforming industrial processes. Additionally, he imparts his knowledge as an adjunct professor at Buffalo State University, mentoring future industry professionals in engineering, leadership, and technology-driven workforce management. His dual perspective as both an industry practitioner and educator provides readers with a comprehensive, forward-looking approach to managing unionized labor in the age of AI.

Index

www.ingramcontent.com/pod-product-compliance
Lightning Source LLC
Chambersburg PA
CBHW061219220326
41599CB00025B/4695